# PRAISE FOR EFFECTIVE NLP SKILLS

WITHDRAWN

'This is a very practical introduction to NLP which avoids too much jargon or faddism. It explains the main tenets of the field and, most importantly, it shows how the NLP may be applied to the most important areas of life, both at work and at home. The subject is clearly explained and should benefit anyone working on either their own development, or the development of others. As a Business Coach, I look forward to the final release of the book.' *Bill Parsons, Executive Vice President, Human Resources, ARM Holdings plc*

'A clear and concise exposition of the practical uses of NLP, both for those self-learning as well for practitioners assisting others in their personal growth. A relevant publication for all professional sectors from the expanding not-for-profit movement to the nation's captains of industry. Dip in and out of it or read it cover to cover – something for everyone.' *Carlo Laurenzi OBE, Chief Executive, London Wildlife Trust*

'If you believe – as I do – that there is more to achieving goals and dreams than ticking boxes, read this book. You will discover an entertaining, easy to follow guide to NLP that will allow you to get the best from yourself, those that you work for and with, and achieve the results you want. My expectations were set at a high level as I began to read this book and I was not disappointed.' *Angela O'Connor, President of the HR Society*

'This is a pragmatic, user-friendly guide that helps you understand NLP; it can be used to improve both your personal and professional lives. Indeed it is a must for everyone's personal development, all aspiring inspirational leaders and anyone for whom building relationships and effective communication are important.' *Mrs Julie Spence OBE QPM, Retired Chief Constable of Cambridgeshire Police*

# EFFECTIVE NLP SKILLS

# CREATING SUCCESS

## The best-selling series is back and better than ever

## MARCH 2013

**Because you only have one chance in life to make a good impression.**

# EFFECTIVE NLP SKILLS

## RICHARD YOUELL, CHRISTINA YOUELL

## CREATING SUCCESS

First published in 2011 by Kogan Page Limited
Second edition 2013,
Reprinted 2014

| | | |
|---|---|---|
| 2nd Floor, 45 Gee Street | 1518 Walnut Street, Suite 1100 | 4737/23 Ansari Road |
| London EC1V 3RS | Philadelphia PA 19102 | Daryaganj |
| United Kingdom | USA | New Delhi 110002 |
| www.koganpage.com | | India |

© Richard Youell & Christina Youell, 2013

The right of Richard Youell & Christina Youell to be identified as the authors of this work has been asserted by them in accordance with the Copyright, Designs and Patents Act 1988.

ISBN      978 0 7494 6704 3
E-ISBN   978 0 7494 6705 0

**British Library Cataloguing-in-Publication Data**

A CIP record for this book is available from the British Library.

**Library of Congress Cataloging-in-Publication Data**

Youell, Richard.
   Effective NLP skills / Richard Youell, Christina Youell. – Second edition.
     pages cm
   Includes bibliographical references.
   ISBN 978-0-7494-6704-3 – ISBN (invalid) 978-0-7494-6705-0 (ebk.)
1. Neurolinguistic programming.   2. Interpersonal communication.   3. Interpersonal relations.   I. Youell, Christina.   II. Title.
   BF637.N46Y68 2013
   158'.9–dc23
                                                                               2012045513

Typeset by Graphicraft Limited, Hong Kong
Printed and bound by CPI Group (UK) Ltd, Croydon, CR0 4YY

# CONTENTS

# Further NLP resources and training opportunities   164

# INTRODUCTION

## WHAT IS NLP?

Have you ever wondered why you find some people difficult or why some people seem to think differently from the way that you do? Have you ever become embroiled in a people problem at work and wondered why you find some people to be challenging or aggressive whilst you experience others as passive or accommodating? Perhaps you have watched a colleague deal successfully with a problem in the team or a customer complaint and you have been curious about how they did that so well? Maybe you have wondered how you could have handled a meeting better or you may want to understand why someone has reacted in a particular way to something that you have said or done. If so, then, it would probably be helpful and useful for you to better understand what is important to them, what drives them and how they operate in the world.

We are all unique individuals who have unique experiences of life and who have made sense of those experiences in our own particular way. This shapes our reactions and the way that we operate in the world.

Neuro-Linguistic Programming (NLP) is 'the study of the structure of subjective experience'. It is concerned with the basic building blocks and functions of our mind–body system that enable us to think, feel, experience and imagine the world around us. NLP describes how we experience the world and people around us (which is what we experience). Knowing something about the structure of the 'how' can be very helpful if we want to make changes to the 'what'.

*Neuro* – this relates to the brain and the things that go on in your mind. It also covers the rest of your neurological system, including your five senses: sight, hearing, feeling, taste and smell.

*Linguistic* – this concerns the language, both spoken and non-spoken (body language) communication systems that you use to code, order and understand the representations that you get from your senses (sights, sounds, feelings, etc) as well as your thoughts and how you make meaning or sense of what you experience.

*Programming* – this concerns your behaviour and thinking patterns, how you organize your thoughts, feelings and communications to achieve your specific desired goals and results. Much of what we do is learnt behaviour, which we perform automatically and unconsciously. In NLP, our thought patterns and behaviours are like computer software programs or scripts that we 'run' in ways that are most useful to us.

Understanding your own programs or scripts can enable you to change these scripts and further develop these programs. Similarly, understanding other people's programs and scripts can help us find better ways to relate to them and interact with them, whether they are the people we manage, our peers or indeed our manager.

## WHEN AND WHERE NLP MIGHT BE USEFUL TO YOU

NLP is a collection of frameworks, models, methodologies and techniques that can help you to better understand yourself and other people. The purpose of the NLP tools and techniques is to have more effective communication, better motivation for yourself and others and a more positive frame of mind. NLP gives you some helpful tools and techniques for changing what you experience and do. It gives you more choices in how you think, feel and behave, so that you have more options to choose from to get what you want. If you want to influence others or get on better with them, you can use these tools and techniques to adapt your behaviour and approach. Often, by changing your behaviour or style you will influence others to change theirs.

There are many contexts in life in which NLP can be helpful. The context that we are most concerned with in this book is the workplace: how you can get the best from yourself and those that you work with, to get the results that you want.

## HOW TO READ THIS BOOK

One of the principles of NLP is the recognition of the benefits of being curious. We ask you, the reader, a number of quetions throughout this book. These questions are born out of our own wanton curiosity and are a great way to get you engaged in your own learning. To get the most benefit from the time you spend reading this book, you will want to consider your responses and reactions to all these questions and reflect on your answers.

Once you have mastered the techniques in this book you will probably want to continue to be curious about yourself and also to develop a curiosity about others.

## THE STRUCTURE OF THIS BOOK

This book is divided into the following chapters. You can dip in and read the book in any order that you like.

### The history, people, influences and development of NLP

A brief summary of the development of NLP, the people involved and their influences and backgrounds.

## Your brain: a user manual

This chapter describes some of the underlying building blocks, frameworks and principles that underpin the NLP tools and techniques described in the other chapters. It describes some fundamental ways in which your neurology works so that you have a better understanding of how you do what you do, so that you can more easily change how you do things, when you want to.

## Managing yourself

This chapter describes some tools and techniques that are useful for managing yourself:

- how you can be very clear about what you want to achieve and how you can better motivate yourself by constructing really compelling goals that you will want to achieve;

- how you can develop a greater awareness of how you think about things, what you believe about the world and how useful or not this is to you;

- how you can choose the most useful attitude or perspective to have in a particular situation;

- how you can develop your own adaptability so that you are better able to act in ways that are most effective for you when situations change.

## Managing others

This chapter describes some tools and techniques that are useful if you manage or need to influence other people at work: how you can build rapport with others so that you can better understand, communicate, influence and motivate them. It gives examples of when to use which tools.

## Powerful use of language

This chapter covers some of the specific tools and techniques that NLP has developed for improving our communications; whether to speak in broad generalizations or whether to be very specific. Body language as well as verbal techniques are addressed here.

## Business applications

This chapter covers some specific workplace situations where NLP techniques can be really useful, such as giving and receiving feedback, conducting appraisals and dealing with poor performance, finding the most appropriate leadership style for a particular situation and selling your ideas and influencing others. It also covers ways in which NLP can be helpful for considering time management and your own levels of stress. These are all examples of where a little NLP know-how and skills can take you a long way.

# THE HISTORY, PEOPLE, INFLUENCES AND DEVELOPMENT OF NLP

## THE EARLY YEARS

Some people find it helpful to have an appreciation of how the field of NLP has developed and the different influences on the key proponents in the field. NLP was developed in the early 1970s at the University of California at Santa Cruz by John Grinder, an associate professor of linguistics, and Richard Bandler, a psychology student with a background in mathematics and computer science. Bandler and Grinder were both interested in how certain people were able to communicate and influence others very effectively. Bringing together Grinder's expertise in language patterns and Bandler's skill in noticing and codifying those patterns, they studied some highly effective therapists who were all able to help people make positive changes to their lives – just by listening to them and talking with them. The therapists that they studied were Fritz Perls, the developer of gestalt therapy, Virginia Satir, a noted specialist in family therapy and change management, and Milton Erickson, an eminent clinical hypnotherapist. These studies, which identified the key behaviours, approaches and language patterns of these therapists, developed into a methodology all of its own, which became NLP. At the heart of this work was the concept of modelling, ie finding a role model, or exemplar, who has an ability to do something very well, observing and questioning them and finding the set of strategies, emotions and behaviours that they use to perform that ability. Once you have identified the components of the ability then others can adopt them and perform that ability.

A team of enthusiastic and visionary friends, many of whom were students at the University of California at the time, further developed and extended the NLP models during the 1970s and 1980s. Robert Dilts, Judith DeLozier, David Gordon, Leslie Cameron Bandler and Steve and Connirae Andreas all worked on extending the NLP models, either independently or together with Bandler and Grinder.

# OTHER INFLUENCES AND THEORIES

In addition to the therapists that Bandler and Grinder modelled, there were some other important influences in the development of NLP.

Gregory Bateson, an eminent anthropologist, linguist and cyberneticist, was at the University of California at the same time as Bandler and Grinder were developing NLP. His work on cybernetics and systems theory influenced the development of NLP and it was Bateson himself who introduced Bandler and Grinder to the hypnotherapist Milton Erikson.

From the field of linguistics, the work of Paul Watzlawick and Noam Chomsky also influenced the development of NLP.

In particular, Watzlawick's works on communication theory and Chomsky's work on transformational grammar were contemporary theories that supported the development of several of the core NLP models.

The field of general semantics, which generalizes the principles of modern scientific thinking and applies them to human activity, also played a large influencing factor in the development of NLP. The work of Alfred Korzybski, particularly that covered in his book *Science and Sanity*, further underpins much of the thinking behind several of the NLP models.

Other scientific research, evidence and theories in both cognitive and behavioural psychology support the NLP models. The works of George Miller, Eugene Galanter and Ivan Pavlov have all had a significant bearing on the development of NLP.

## NLP: A MODEL, NOT A THEORY

NLP was developed by modelling what successful communicators did and how they did it, rather than why they did what they did. This is an important distinction and is different from many other methodologies which rely on an underlying theory of why something works. As a model-based methodology it does not have to be completely 'true', 'correct' or even 'consistent'. What is most important is whether or not it works. Model-based methodologies like NLP are only useful when applied to what they were originally designed for. This has led to an approach in NLP which says 'If it works, use it. If it doesn't, then try something else', and 'This always works – except when it doesn't'. It can be helpful to appreciate this ethos when using NLP as there is rarely one single methodology that is sure to work in all situations for all people. The NLP models provide a helpful framework for choosing which approaches to take and developing the flexibility to try those different approaches, to get the results that you want. You can try out the tools and adopt the techniques and methods that work for you.

# RECENT HISTORY

During the 1980s the collaboration between Bandler and Grinder ended abruptly in a series of public disagreements, controversies and law suits. A partial resolution to some of the disagreements was agreed between the two in the late 1990s. However, the legal issues surrounding intellectual property ownership of the original NLP models were never completely resolved and two decades of ongoing disputes resulted in the field of NLP becoming the fragmented and diverse 'discipline' that it is today.

Many of the early team from Santa Cruz, including John Grinder, Robert Dilts and David Gordon, have continued to develop, publish and train NLP in various guises. At the same time, others have taken the basic principles and models developed in the 1970s and added, modified, updated, renamed and rebranded the early work into new branches of human communication, behaviour, management and change. For example, developers like Steven Covey (1989), Tony Robbins (1986, 1992) and Ken Blanchard and Spencer Johnson (1983) have all developed their own models and methodologies that appear to have many of the early NLP principles at their core.

Today there are many 'brands' of NLP, and each trainer, writer and practitioner will emphasize their own particular style, based on their own experiences and learning. While some practitioners focus exclusively on the application of NLP to personal development or therapeutic skills, others are more interested in the application of NLP in a business and organizational context. The authors believe that an understanding of people, both oneself and others, together with some practised and effective self-management skills, is a necessary prerequisite for communicating with and leading other people effectively in such a business context. Most of the examples given in this book relate to business situations.

# SUMMARY

- Richard Bandler, a computer scientist studying psychology, and John Grinder, an associate professor of linguistics at the University of California in Santa Cruz collaborated on the early development of NLP in the 1970s.

- NLP studies and models useful abilities that people do well, so that others can chose to develop the same strategies, states and behaviours and acquire the useful ability themselves.

- NLP is not concerned with the theory of 'why' particular behaviours can be effective, rather it is about 'how' to behave in those useful ways.

- Of particular interest to Bandler and Grinder, when they developed NLP, was the ability to communicate and influence.

# YOUR BRAIN: A USER MANUAL

**A mind is like a parachute. It doesn't work if it's not open.**
FRANK ZAPPA

Have you ever done something and wondered, 'How did I do that?', or 'Why do I keep doing that?' Understanding how our mind works can help us use our mind better to achieve our goals. It can also give us choices about how we use our brain.

The human brain is an incredibly complex and adaptive organ. Its ability to process and make sense of the huge amount of information that it receives from our senses and the varied and complex experiences we undertake as we go through life is quite amazing. We are not usually conscious of how our brain works; how we learn a new skill, change our attitude or how we feel, invoke a search of our own memories, mentally rehearse a future situation or react to certain events in a particular way. These things often 'just happen', automatically and unconsciously. Because these processes happen unconsciously, some people assume that nothing can be done to change how we do things. However, by understanding how the brain works we can develop new strategies that serve us better than current approaches.

Recent advances in technology have enabled neuroscientists to make significant discoveries about how the brain and mind work. Techniques such as MRI scanning and PET imaging have pushed forward our understanding of the brain and mind. Of particular note is the discovery of the brain's ability to change its physical structure (anatomy) as well as its functional organization in response to learning, thinking and experience, a phenomenon called 'neuroplasticity'.

Many of the techniques and methodologies in NLP utilize the basic structures and neurological building blocks that we already possess as part of our mind–body system. Having some understanding of how to engage and utilize these basic structures and neurological building blocks allows us to more consciously and purposefully make the adaptations, skill developments and changes that we want to how we think, feel and react, rather than just relying on our 'automatic' or unconscious ability to make changes. It is rather like getting the user manual for the brain and developing new, more useful software that we can choose to run when our standard or automatic software isn't working well for us. Of course, like changing any software, it's a good idea if we are able to test and configure it to suit our specific purpose and be able to go back to an older version if and when we want to. Fortunately, NLP has some procedures and methodologies that allow us to do that too.

## ACTIVITY  WHAT WOULD YOU DO WITH THE USER MANUAL FOR YOUR BRAIN?

- What would it be like if you had the user manual for your brain? Which section of the manual would you look at first?

- What if you knew how to access and make best use of the indexing system that your brain preferred to use for filing away dim and distant memories?

- What if you knew how your own mind–body system motivates itself to do the things that you wanted?

- What programs do you run 'automatically' that don't always serve you well? What would you like to do or feel differently instead?

- What if you could quickly and easily choose different reactions to situations?

- Which new ability would you learn first?

# LEARNING AND DEVELOPING HABITS

**I am always doing that which I cannot do,
in order that I may learn how to do it.**
PABLO PICASSO

Understanding how we learn can help us learn more efficiently and this can be very helpful when time is short and we want to be the best that we can be. I've never met anybody who had finished learning. Continually learning and adapting is a basic survival mechanism that has helped us evolve to be who we are today.

## What is learning?

As soon as we are born we start the process of learning how to do things and how not to do them. Human beings are fabulous learning machines. Often, what we learn soon becomes second nature and we do what we have learnt automatically, without even thinking about it. We don't need to think about how to walk, talk, answer the phone or drive from home to work. Once we have learnt how to do it, it all just happens, unconsciously. The same is true of how we behave in certain situations and circumstances. Our actions and reactions are learnt behaviours that are run automatically, out of habit and usually completely unconsciously.

## Continuous learning

Everything that we have learnt has been useful to us in some situation or context – even when it's how not to behave or what not to do. And while that action or behaviour continues to be effective and helpful, you don't even need to think about what to do, you just do it. However, when the situation or context changes, you might find that what you usually do doesn't work so well for you. Then learning a different, more useful way of acting or behaving can be very helpful.

An old proverb says 'If you always do what you have always done, then you will always get what you always got'. This is fine if you are getting what you want but not if you are getting an undesired result.

Learning how we learn, and how we develop these automatic habits, can be helpful when we want to learn new things or develop new skills, habits and behaviours. Understanding our own learning process can help us to learn more easily and effectively.

## How we learn

The learning cycle in Figure 2.1 represents the cycle of how we learn new abilities and reactions. One side represents whether we are competent at a skill or ability or incompetent at what we are doing. The other side represents whether we know what we are doing, whether we are conscious or unconscious of how we are doing it.

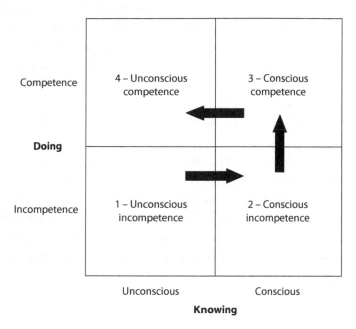

**Competence**

4 – Unconscious competence

3 – Conscious competence

**Doing**

**Incompetence**

1 – Unconscious incompetence

2 – Conscious incompetence

Unconscious

Conscious

**Knowing**

**Figure 2.1**   The learning cycle

We usually start in a state of not knowing what we don't know, called 'unconscious incompetence'. If we have never done something, probably because we have not needed to or desired to, then we have probably not even considered either the possibility of doing it or how we might do it. When I was a small child I never considered that driving a car was something that I would learn in later life. Driving a car was just something that grown-ups did. However, at the beginning of my first driving lesson, I quickly moved to the next stage of the learning cycle, called 'conscious incompetence'. As the car leapt and weaved its way down the road, the engine stalled and we rolled into the kerb. I became very aware of my own incompetence. I felt very foolish at the time but was determined to learn how to drive. I wanted the freedom that came with having a driving licence. Gradually, as the driving lessons progressed, I moved into stage 3 of the learning cycle, as shown in Figure 2.1. As I recited to myself 'Mirror, signal, manoeuvre', and learnt the technique of easing off the accelerator, depressing the clutch, changing gear and then slowly lifting the clutch while depressing the accelerator I became very conscious of my developing competence – albeit with the occasional and rather embarrassing visit back to stages 1 and 2. During my driving test I was completely absorbed with the techniques and skills I had learnt – it took all of my conscious effort – and I passed.

Many years later, and after many miles of driving I have become an unconsciously competent driver. I still sometimes wonder how I know when a car in front of me is going to make that unusual manoeuvre that I seem to have anticipated, how I managed that hill start without reciting my 'script' and how I managed to end up safely at my usual destination without having been aware either of driving the car or of the journey itself.

## Continuing the continuous learning

**Enlightenment is always preceded by confusion.**
MILTON H ERICKSON

Several years ago, when I did a job that required that I drive lots of miles to meet clients and business partners, my then employer sent me on a defensive driving course. I had passed my driving test almost a decade previously and now spent most of my driving time in 'unconscious competence'. I did not need to think very much or hard about how to drive and thought that I was a fairly good driver. On the defensive driving course my instructor pointed out lots of bad and potentially dangerous habits that I had developed and taught me a good number of new techniques and things to be aware of that I hadn't noticed before. I had thought that I was firmly at stage 4 and yet the course had made me realize that much of what I was doing was actually in stage 1 of the cycle, back in unconscious incompetence. I had become complacent and needed to develop some new skills and awareness. Many of the habits that I had developed seemed to be difficult to break. I had to go through the whole learning process again, not just on the day of the course. I needed to make learning how to drive safely and effectively a continuous learning process.

## ACTIVITY EXPLORING YOUR OWN LEARNING

- Like the example of learning to drive, you will have similar experiences of learning new skills and abilities. How do you recognize which of the four stages of learning you are in?

- What behaviours and reactions to situations do you currently carry out automatically and unconsciously? Are they effective? Are they giving you the outcomes that you want? If not, what needs to happen for you to develop some alternative behaviours and reactions that might serve you better?

- What would it take for you to become aware of any incompetence or ineffectiveness in the way that you do things? What could you do to speed up the process of improving your learning?

- When you have learnt things in the past, what feelings did you experience as you moved from stage 1 to stages 2 and 3 of the learning cycle? Those feelings can provide good markers that signal where you are in the process of learning. How could you use those feelings to help chart your progress and motivate yourself as you learn new skills? Are there any feelings that get in the way of you learning new things, improving your existing skills, or that are keeping you stuck at a particular stage?

# COMING TO YOUR SENSES: REPRESENTATIONAL SYSTEMS AND SUBMODALITIES

Have you ever been to a conference, listened to a speaker and then discussed what you heard with a colleague who listened to the same speaker? Often when people do this they find that the other person has heard different things or remembers different bits of the presentation. Sometimes these can be so different that you can wonder whether you were listening to the same speaker! This happens because we all have different preferences in the way that we take in and process information. Understanding this can be very helpful when you need to get an important business message across to a number of people.

## What are representational systems?

Human beings have five ways of getting information from the outside world into our inner world of experience, understanding, perception and memory. Our eyes see what is going on around us and we convert the information from our eyes into images that we can process, experience and hold in our memory. Similarly, we can hear, feel or touch, taste and smell what is going on around us and process and store that information. The NLP term for these five channels of information is 'representational systems', often shortened to 'rep systems'. Our rep systems are how we represent the world to our inner selves:

- Visual (V) – what we see;

- Auditory (A) – what we hear;

- Kinaesthetic (K) – what we feel;

- Olfactory (O) – what we smell;

- Gustatory (G) – what we taste.

We usually concentrate on only the first three rep systems – V, A and K – as they are the most useful in a business context.

## What are submodalities?

Each rep system can be divided into a series of subjective distinctions that are used to describe what is sensed. For the V rep system for example, we have lightness, monochrome or colour, hue, focus, near or far. For the A rep system, sounds can have different pitch, timbre, clarity and loudness. Finally, for the K rep system we have temperature, texture, hard or soft, etc. The different submodalities or qualities of each rep system are how we have coded the sensory information and use it in our minds. When you see a tomato do you experience the same colour, red, as everyone else sees, or do we all have a different perception of red?

## Why are rep systems and submodalities important?

The rep systems provide the basic building blocks of how we experience and perceive the world around us. Using sensory-specific language (what we see, hear and feel) provides a way of speaking in the 'lowest common denominator', which can be universally motivating and influential. Rather than talking in abstractions about concepts and theories, using sensory-specific language often gives the best chance of being understood by others.

We usually have a preference for one rep system over the others in many situations. This will influence how important that information is to our perceptions or how much we trust information from that rep system compared with the other systems. Knowing that these preferences exist for ourselves and other people can be utilized in ways that are useful when communicating with them.

Changing submodalities is a very effective and powerful way of changing the meaning of an experience. For example, you can change the way you feel about something and the intensity of that feeling by altering the submodalities associated with it. For many people there are 'critical' submodalities that can completely change their perceptions of an experience or memory in ways that are helpful to them. Often memories which are brighter and more colourful are more compelling and give rise to 'good' feelings as opposed to those memories which are dark or monochrome and give rise to 'bad' feelings or memories. Of course, changing submodalities is not changing the content of the experience or memory (what actually happened), just the way that your brain has decided to code the information that you received from your senses.

## Noticing rep systems

Some people have a preference for a particular rep system compared with the others. You can tell this from the language they use to describe their experience. For individuals with a clear preference, information from their preferred rep system, either V, A or K, will have more 'weight' or meaning than the information from the other systems. If they receive conflicting signals from their rep systems then they are more likely to trust the information from their preferred rep system over that from their non-preferred systems. For example, for some people, 'seeing is believing'; others might not be so convinced until things 'sound right' to them or 'ring true'; and a third group might only be persuaded when they feel that something is 'just right'. A good way to detect any such preferences is by noticing the language that the person uses in a particular situation. The open question, 'What did you notice?' can be used to elicit any such preferences. Listen carefully to the reply and notice what rep systems are used.

I once worked with a colleague who I found difficult to understand. When I listened carefully to what she said I realized that she spoke in auditory language whilst my preference is visual language. She would say things like 'I need to say, that the team are squawking about this issue and they need more time to tune in to the customers' priorities' and I would think 'Why can't you be clear about the problem and show me a plan that sets out transparently what you can see needs doing?' It was not until I developed some flexibility to match her language with the same sensory language that I was able to better understand what she was saying.

The way that information is taken in to the system is often the same way that the information is stored and therefore being able to decode a person's sensory preference for receiving information can help us 'talk their language'. This can be very helpful in negotiations or when giving feedback, which are situations where you generally want to communicate effectively and avoid any misunderstanding. This can be achieved by speaking in the same sensory-specific language as the person you are in dialogue with.

## Some visual words

Table 2.1

| SEE | LOOK | HORIZON | LANDSCAPE | PICTURE | VIEW | BRIGHT |
|-----|------|---------|-----------|---------|------|--------|
| view | sparkle | colour | colour | show | focus | perspective |
| colourful | bright | appears | hazy | light | reveal | vision |
| illuminate | clear | foggy | cloudy | flash | fade | vivid |

## Some visual phrases

an eyeful...

Can you show me what you mean?

catch a glimpse of...

dim view...

He has a bright future.

He uses colourful language.

I get the picture.

I have an insight into how to look at things from his perspective.

in light of...

I see what you mean.

mind's eye...

Things are looking good.

tunnel vision...

We need to focus.

## Some auditory words

Table 2.2

| rhythm | song | book | tone | timbre | clash | thunder |
|---|---|---|---|---|---|---|
| sounds | harmony | listen | hear | discuss | speak | chimes |
| voiced | listen | resonate | deaf | question | silence | announce |

## Some auditory phrases

clear as a bell...

I hear what you say.

I like the sound of that.

in tune...

power of speech...

rings a bell...

strike a chord...

tongue tied...

tuned in...

voiced an opinion...

### Some kinaesthetic words

Table 2.3

| feel | smooth | pulse | touch | cool | grasp |
|------|--------|-------|-------|------|-------|
| throw | turn | hard | unfeeling | concrete | scrape |
| impression | contact | hold | tap | solid | catch |

### Some kinaesthetic phrases

boils down to...

get in touch with...

get to grips with...

hold on...

in control...

pain in the neck...

pull some strings...

start from scratch...

stiff upper lip...

too much hassle...

# Preferences

Some people don't have a strong rep system preference and yet others do. Also, people's preferences can change depending on the situation or context – they might prefer to use lots of V language for discussions about how things seem to them at a progress or technical-review meeting and yet will prefer to use K language when describing an experience in a different setting or context.

## Building rapport by using the same rep system

Once you have detected that someone has a preference for a particular rep system, then, if you use that same rep system yourself your communications with them are likely to be more effective:

- you will be seeing eye to eye (V);

- singing from the same song book (A);

- on the same page (K).

However, if you use a different rep system from their preferred system, you are more likely to:

- distract them from their focus of attention (V);

- clash with them (A);

- rub them up the wrong way (K).

Very often, people who have difficulties communicating with each other, showing empathy or building rapport are simply mismatching each other's rep systems. Does that ring true for you? How does that idea grab you? Do you see what I mean? Of course, if you are communicating with a team or group of people, it's a good idea to utilize all three rep systems rather than simply rely on your own preference to ensure that you are speaking to all of them effectively. This requires you to develop the flexibility to use all the rep systems in your language. This can be particularly important when you are communicating to a number of people such as when making company announcements, or presentations, and when writing marketing literature.

# Changing perceptions by using submodality shifts

Many of the early NLP techniques and procedures developed by Bandler and Grinder for changing perceptions and meanings used submodality shifts. Many of these techniques are still used by coaches and therapists when someone wants to feel differently from (better than) how they currently do about a situation or experience. A useful way that submodality shifts can be used in the workplace is to consider two contrasting situations or experiences and notice the submodality differences between the two. Individuals will usually find that one or two submodality shifts will completely change their perception of the experience. These are called the 'critical submodalities' and are useful levers for changing perceptions. Of course, the critical shifts might well be different for different individuals.

Suppose you were involved in a change at work, such as a change in working practices, procedures or a new office layout. These can often be met with considerable resistance.

Noticing the submodalities of the current situation and contrasting them with the submodalities of the future situation can be enlightening. How do you perceive the current arrangements and compare that with how you imagine things will be after the change? What submodality shifts do you notice? Perhaps one situation is louder, nearer, more vivid or colourful, warmer, cooler, brighter or completely monochrome. Does one have a border around it? Is one a film, the other a still picture? Perhaps one situation has a different tone to it or a different feel. Now take the submodalities of the 'better' situation and apply them to the 'worse' situation. Modify the pictures, sounds and feelings of the 'bad' situation by giving them the same submodalities as the 'good' situation and notice how you perceive that situation now. Be careful not to alter the content of the situation, just the coding of the submodalities. You can try this on your own at first, before you get your colleagues to say what submodality shifts would make the situation better for them, even as the content stays the same.

Lara used this approach when she conducted a follow-up meeting with a client following a previous meeting which had not gone well. In order to do this, she reflected on the ways that she recalled the first meeting in her memory: the room was dark with no natural light; it was cold and she was feeling nervous about how the individual would react to what she had to say, which made her voice sound shaky. She contrasted this with another meeting where there was plenty of natural light; with the sun shining in. It was warm and she felt relaxed. Her voice sounded normal.

She then took the sunshine and her voice sounding normal (the two critical submodalities for her in this instance) from her memory of the good meeting in to her memory of the not-so-good meetings and found that she felt better. This enabled her to feel more relaxed about the follow-up meeting and to therefore approach the situation in a more helpful state.

# ACTIVITY BECOMING AWARE OF YOUR SENSES

- Become consciously aware of the rep systems that your colleagues prefer to use at work in certain situations. Practise matching your responses in the same rep system and notice the responses you get in return.

- Develop an awareness of your own rep system preferences. Practise using language that uses your non-preferred rep systems to improve the effectiveness of your communications with others who might not share your preferences.

Notice how much more rapport you can build, particularly with those that you have previously not been able to.

- Which are your critical submodalities? What changes do you need to make to how you perceive situations to really motivate yourself to do those things that you have been putting off for so long now?

- What happens when you take the submodalities of a situation that you clearly understand and apply them to some content that you are currently confused about? What happens to the structure of the content and the confusion?

# OUTCOME THINKING

Alice came to a fork in the road.
'Which road do I take?' she asked.
'Where do you want to go?' responded the Cheshire cat.
'I don't know,' Alice answered.
'Then,' said the cat, 'it doesn't matter.'
LEWIS CARROLL

If you don't know where you are going... how will you know that you have got there? It is really helpful to be able to state what you want. Some people find it easy to do this. Others find that they more naturally state what they don't want or what they want to avoid and find it much harder to state what they do want. In business, we need to be able to do both. We need to be able to set out our business plans and objectives whilst also paying attention to the risks associated with our plans (the things we don't want to happen).

## What is outcome thinking?

Outcome thinking is simply thinking about what you do want rather than what you don't want. This is sometimes called 'towards' thinking rather than 'away-from' thinking. Some people tend to use towards thinking in their life and others tend to use away-from thinking. Both can be useful in a business context and it is helpful to understand the difference between them.

## When is outcome thinking helpful?

The brain is not very good at dealing with negative statements. In order not to do something our minds have to come up with a representation of doing it and then try and not do this!

## ACTIVITY  NEGATIVE STATEMENTS

Spend the next 20 seconds not thinking of Elvis.

*What did you do?*

We gave your mind a representation of the very thing you were trying not to think of: Elvis. Think how much more difficult it would have been had we included a picture of Elvis on this page or hummed the tune of 'Hound Dog' just before you started the activity. In order to make sense of the instruction, your brain deletes the word 'not' and creates a representation of what it needs to move away from. This explains why a child will often spill their drink just after they have been told 'Don't spill your drink'. Saying something like 'Be careful with your drink' helps the child focus on being careful rather than spilling. 'Don't look down!' is another example of a statement that compels you to look down.

## Towards and away-from thinking: the two directions of motivation

If we have a tendency to focus on things we don't want we call this 'away-from thinking'. If we have a tendency to focus on what we do want we call this 'towards thinking'. Away-from thinking can be useful when you need to get out of a situation quickly. It invokes the body's inbuilt survival flight-or-fight response. However, it can be rather like jumping into a taxi and on hearing the driver say 'Where do you want to go?' replying 'Out of here!' This is not very helpful for you or the driver. However, away-from thinking can be very useful in the event of a fire or when you are identifying the risks linked to a project.

Towards and away-from thinking are two opposite motivations; they are how we get ourselves to do things. It is helpful to recognize the difference between the two as they act in different ways. Away-from thinking is great when there is a risk or danger and you need to be motivated to do something quickly. Your body's flight-or-fight response ensures that when you are motivated in this way, hormones such as adrenaline and cortisol raise your heart rate and levels of alertness to help you react quickly. Although it is often a very effective motivator, away-from thinking can sometimes lead to short-term actions that are not always sustained over the long term and if overused can cause stress and anxiety. Towards thinking, on the other hand, requires you to use your imagination, can be a much better long-term motivator and is usually a much less stressful way of getting something done. In old-style management books these two motivators are often referred to as 'carrot' and 'stick' methods.

Understanding whether someone has a preference for away-from thinking or towards thinking can be very useful if you are trying to influence or sell to them. You can usually spot their preference in the language patterns that they use. Do they say that they 'do want' or 'don't want' something? To most effectively influence them, simply match your response to their preferred direction of travel. If someone tells you what they don't want to happen, you can reassure them that the product or service you are selling will help prevent that from happening. If they tell you what they do want to happen, you can explain how your product or service will help them ensure that it does.

In a business context the two different approaches work well when managing a project. It is important to set out what the project outcomes are; what successful completion of the project will give the business. It is also helpful to set out the milestones of what needs to happen in order to achieve this. Alongside this, the project plan also needs to consider all the risks and problems that may occur along the way. A business made up of only 'towards thinkers' would soon encounter problems or risks that were not anticipated in the planning stage because no one was thinking about potential problems. A business comprising of only 'away from' thinkers may never get off the ground because everyone is thinking about the potential problems and not about what they do want to have happen.

## Making effective use of your imagination

To invoke towards thinking, you need to create in your mind a reference point for what you want; whether this is a performance objective, a business development plan or to simply conclude a meeting on time. Sometimes this can be recalling what has happened in the past that you want to happen again (a memory) or it could be imagining what you want to happen, that hasn't happened before. The mind finds it difficult to tell the difference between a thought that is remembered and one that is imagined, and therefore either approach is a powerful way of training your mind to focus on what you do want. It helps if you make the vision of what you do want rich and vivid in sensory-specific terms. What will you see, hear and feel when you have what you want? How will you know you have reached your outcome? What evidence will there be?

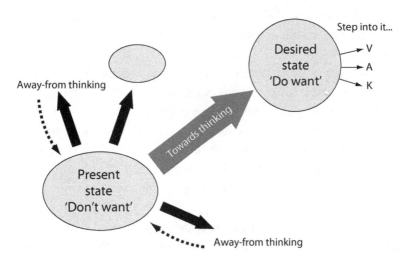

**Figure 2.2**  Outcome thinking

Now that you have a representation of what you do want, your mind will start to look for this and it will recognize it when it finds it; the vivid reference point you have imagined becomes like a target (see Figure 2.2). The more detailed you make your representation, the more compelling it becomes and the more likely you are to move towards it. This evidence also tells your mind when you have reached your goal and your outcome is achieved. The empty balloon represents a state which isn't what you 'Don't want' but isn't what you 'Do want' either. It's where many people end up when they try hard to move away from something that they don't want without thinking about what they do want instead. It's usually not what they want at all – and no better (sometimes worse) than what they moved away from.

Think of something that you want at work. What would you like to have happen? Step into your desired outcome. Go there for a moment. Act as if it has already happened and make it vivid and richly sensory specific. Notice what you would see inside and outside yourself. What would you hear yourself and others saying? How would you feel if you had achieved your outcome? The answers to these questions give you the evidence of your outcome.

The same sort of thinking can help you achieve your career ambitions and is used to help companies achieve their objectives by having a compelling vision with evidence of what they will see, hear and feel when the vision is achieved. Outcome thinking is often much more effective than thinking about all the terrible things that you don't want to have happen, as well as being a much more pleasant and sustainable way of motivating yourself and others.

Teams that invest a little time to develop a shared vision of how they want the business to develop tend to achieve their vision more effectively than those that are unclear about their goal. This is because they have expressed the evidence of how they would know that they were achieving their vision in terms of what they would see, hear and feel and because they use this evidence to guide their actions and decisions.

## CASE STUDY

Paul was frustrated that a product that he had ordered for an important client had still not been delivered. He rang the company to find out what the problem was.

Before he made the call he took a deep breath and focused on his outcome; he wanted the product to be delivered as soon as possible. He was tempted to shout at the sales person who answered the phone and to tell them how incompetent he thought they were. However he knew that this was unlikely to be helpful as the sales person would probably become defensive and may not be prepared to help him.

▶

Paul made the call and explained to the sales person that he had ordered the product for an important client and it hadn't arrived as promised. He asked the sales person how they could help him serve his customer.

The sales person acknowledged that there had been a delay, apologized and agreed to dispatch the product direct to the customer next-day delivery at no extra cost. Paul thanked the sales person. He had got his outcome.

## ACTIVITY PUTTING OUTCOME THINKING INTO PRACTICE

- Start to pay attention to how often you think about what you do want and how often you think about what you don't want, so that you understand your own preferences and self-motivations. Are those preferences serving you well? Do they get you motivated rapidly enough and help you achieve your goals?

- You can use towards thinking to help prepare for a meeting that you want to go well. Imagine what the meeting would be like when things go well. What will you be doing? How will you feel? What would people be saying and what will you be hearing yourself say... go there and experience this in your mind before the meeting.

- Have you noticed that some people come to you with their problems and list all the things they want to avoid happening? Sometimes people can get very stuck in this pattern of thinking, which can be very unhelpful for them.

What if you helped them flip their thinking from away-from to towards? 'What would you like to have happen?' is a great question for doing that. 'What would you like to see, hear and feel instead?' is another. Notice their response. If away-from thinking is their preference, you might need to help them some more by increasing your curiosity and making sure that you are in rapport.

# PATTERNS OF THINKING AND PREFERENCES

Everything that irritates us about others can lead us to an understanding of ourselves.
CARL JUNG

In business we meet all sorts of people; some of whom appear to think just like us and to be very sensible and normal and others who think differently to us and who we can sometimes perceive to be difficult or awkward. This happens because people can have different preferences in the way they take in information and in the way that they think. Because it is different from our way of doing things and we think of ourselves as pretty normal, we can sometimes judge people with different thinking patterns to be 'not normal' when what we mean is they are just different from us. Understanding types of difference in thinking patterns can help us work out what we need to do to build a better relationship or communicate more effectively with someone who thinks differently from us.

## What are patterns of thinking?

We all have our own favourite ways of doing things. We even have our own favourite ways of thinking. This is part of how we learn and act in the world. When something works for us in a particular situation we will usually try doing it that way again when faced with a similar situation. Soon it becomes an automatic habit. We prefer to always do things that way. It saves us the time and effort of thinking about how to do something each time we are faced with a problem. By the time we are young adults, we have developed a well-tried and tested set of thinking patterns (just like a toolkit), some of these thinking patterns or tools we will prefer to use more often than others.

## When is understanding patterns of thinking useful?

Knowing your own preferred patterns of thinking and behaviour can help you understand how and why you sometimes approach and experience situations differently from other people. Knowing your own thinking preferences will also help you understand which non-preferred patterns might be useful to develop and use in certain situations. Developing this flexibility can be very useful when what usually works for you is currently not working or not working as well as you would like.

Your thinking patterns and preferences are rather like being left or right-handed. You probably prefer to write your signature and perform certain tasks with one hand or the other. Using the 'wrong' hand requires more effort, feels clumsy and often the result might look clumsy too. However, neither hand is inherently any better than the other for performing tasks such as writing, just more practised. It can sometimes be useful to be able to use your non-preferred hand to do things in particular situations.

Noticing other people's patterns of thinking can be helpful too. If you know how someone else prefers to think about something, or how they prefer to understand a situation or issue, that will give you an indication of how you can best communicate with them, build rapport, influence them or reach a better mutual understanding.

Research indicates that diverse teams are more effective than teams comprised of people with similar thinking patterns. This might be because the more perspectives on a business problem the more solutions become apparent. The greater the range of thinking the more information is available to the team. Therefore, it is helpful to build diverse teams and to be able to work with people with a variety of thinking patterns.

## Some well-known patterns of thinking

Perhaps the most famous thinking patterns are those proposed by Carl Jung and developed into the Myers-Briggs Type Indicator (MBTI®). Jung's theory was that differences in behaviour were the result of people's inborn tendencies to use their minds in different ways. The MBTI system has four pairs of thinking patterns where individuals have a preference for one or other of the pair in each pattern.

### Taking in information

Jung observed that people prefer to have one of two ways of taking in information from the outside world. Some prefer to attend to specific facts and details of what is actually happening in the here and now, called 'sensing' in MBTI, while others prefer to attend to patterns and associations between the facts rather than the facts themselves, called 'intuitive' in MBTI. Those with an intuitive preference usually focus on the 'big picture' and enjoy anticipating the future, while those with a sensing preference usually notice the details and will often compare what they see with past experiences.

### Making decisions

Jung also observed that people have two different ways of making decisions and that there is often a preference towards one or the other. Those with a thinking preference will make their decisions based on objective fact and logic, usually from a detached standpoint. Those with a feeling preference tend to make their decisions from an involved viewpoint and will be guided by their personal values and convictions while considering the impact of their decision on others.

### Focus of attention

Jung also noticed that there are two different directions in which people prefer to focus their energy and attention. Those with an introverted preference have a focus on their internal world of thought and ideas and usually prefer to think through and reflect on issues before discussing them. Those with an extroverted preference, on the other hand, focus their energy and attention on the outside world. They usually prefer to talk through issues with others first and prefer to get involved with activities and events.

### Lifestyle and time

The final MBTI patterns are about how people prefer to deal with the world around them, particularly their relationship with time. Those with a judging preference like to come to closure on issues and lead their lives in a scheduled and ordered way. They like to make plans and stick to them until things are completed. Those with a perceiving preference, on the other hand, like to live their lives in a more flexible and spontaneous way. They are more comfortable going with the flow and adapting to new situations by keeping their options open as long as possible.

## Metaprograms: some other patterns of thinking

The early developers of NLP liked the Myers-Briggs system and the idea that people have preferred patterns of thinking. They extended the list of patterns of thinking into what in NLP are called the 'metaprograms'. Table 2.4 shows a few of the NLP metaprograms.

## Finding out preferences

Of course, you could complete a Myers-Briggs questionnaire or other such psychometric instrument which would give you a

**Table 2.4** NLP metaprograms

| Towards | Away from |
|---|---|
| Focus on what they do want. | Focus on what they don't want. |
| Natural outcome thinkers and visionaries. | Start from what they want to avoid or exclude. Look for problems or potential problems. Great at risk management. |

| Match | Mismatch |
|---|---|
| Will align themselves with others. Will get in tune with others' mood and thinking. | More likely to engage and show interest by challenging and questioning. |

| Internally referenced | Externally referenced |
|---|---|
| Have their own internal standards and are their own judges. Know when they have done something well or poorly. | Look to others for feedback on performance. Trust others' feedback more than their own perceptions of how well they have done. |

| Sameness | Difference |
|---|---|
| Look for how something is like other things they know already. | Notice what is different and seek out things that are different. |

| Past | Present | Future |
|---|---|---|
| Will relate everything to how it used to be. | Live in the moment; may not plan for the future nor learn from previous experience. | Major focus on planning; may not pay enough attention to now. |

statistically valid and reliable method of determining your preferences. However, you probably have a good idea about your own patterns of thinking preferences now that you have seen some of the Myers-Briggs and metaprogram pairs. You might even be able to have a good guess at some of the preferences of your work colleagues. Many of them can be deduced by observing how you and others carry out your workplace tasks and interact with others. Many of the preferences can be found out with simple, conversational questioning:

- 'What would be your ideal weekend?' would be a good question to elicit whether someone had a preferred focus of attention which was introverted (perhaps a quiet time away in the countryside with a loved one) or extroverted (playing team sports and lots of socializing with others).

- 'What information do you need before setting out on a long journey?' would help you discover whether someone had a preference for sensing (would need maps, routes, GPS information, etc) or intuitive patterns (more likely to feel that they have a good sense of direction and know roughly which route to take).

- Asking someone about how they made a recent important decision might help you discover if they had a thinking or feeling preference. Did they weigh up all the pros and cons or did they step into the situation and do the thing that felt right at the time?

- 'How do you know you have done a good job?' is likely to tell you if someone prefers to trust their own internal reference (what they know to be true themselves) or an external reference (feedback from someone else carries more weight than their own opinions).

Your experience of someone with a different thinking pattern will often be positive. I have a preference for the big picture and when I need someone to review a presentation I always go to someone with a preference for detail to make sure that they pick up any mistakes that I may have overlooked. They come to me when they have become bogged down in the details to help them see the big picture and to reconnect with the overall aims of the business.

Your experience of someone with a different thinking pattern may also be less than positive; 'Why do you focus on whether I have used my apostrophes correctly when I am asking you to sign off the outline vision for the business for the next five years?' It can be helpful to focus on the added value of a different thinking pattern and to remember that our thinking patterns are our preferences rather than our attempts to irritate or frustrate others!

# ACTIVITY USING YOUR UNDERSTANDING OF PREFERENCES

- Start to notice the language used by yourself and others that gives indications about thinking patterns. Asking 'What's important about that?' can give further insights into preferred patterns of thinking.

- If you have someone with whom you would like to be able to communicate better and influence, pay particular attention to their patterns of thinking. If you adopt similar patterns to theirs you will be able to build much better rapport with them. For example, if they have a preference for spontaneity and keeping their options open, then you might want to point out the places in your carefully constructed plan where different options and possibilities can be reviewed, considered and potentially accommodated.

- Often, when we get that 'Here we go again' feeling, it is because the same old preferred patterns of thinking and behaviour are being replayed. Next time you get that feeling, why not think about what preferences you are automatically performing and stretch into the opposite pattern. For example, if you are confused about something and you normally like to think things through before sharing your ideas (an introverted preference), you might like to try discussing it with someone else or even a large group of people before you decide for yourself. Of course, like using your non-preferred hand to do something, it might feel a little unusual at first, and might even feel a little clumsy. You will be building your flexibility and capabilities to become competent in new patterns of thinking which you can choose to use, to serve you well in the future.

# MIND–BODY, IMAGINATION AND TIME

Imagination is more important than knowledge. For knowledge is limited to all we now know and understand, while imagination embraces the entire world, and all there ever will be to know and understand.

ALBERT EINSTEIN

Understanding the link between what we think and what we feel can give us greater insight into what works well for us and what works less well. Starting a potentially challenging meeting when you are hungry or tired is probably not an ideal way to ensure clear thinking and a productive meeting. Appreciating this can help us optimize our performance by making sure that we pay attention to the needs of both the body and the mind.

## Your mind–body

NLP has a systemic view of the mind–body. Taking a systemic view is the process of understanding how different components within a system influence one another and the relationships between all the components rather than considering each component on its own in a simple, linear system with cause and effect linkages. Specifically, in NLP we hold the belief that *mind and body are part of the same system and anything that occurs in one part of the system will affect the other.*

You might have noticed that how you feel can influence how you think or experience a situation. If you are feeling tired, have toothache or a hangover, then your experience of a long meeting, a loud repetitive noise or your ability to notice what is going on around you are likely to be very different than if you were alert and without pain. You might also have noticed that your responses to situations are different depending on how you feel. Similarly, you will have noticed that you can often get a good understanding of how someone is feeling before they even get a chance to tell you, by their body language and general demeanour.

We have all been in meetings that have gone on for too long. Have you noticed how meetings drag when you are hungry and how that can lead you to become impatient with others who seem to talk for too long and how that causes you to fidget and lose concentration. That is an example of one part of the system (our stomach) impacting on the mind.

We have probably also all experienced a day which flew by, where we forgot to have lunch because we were so engrossed in a piece of work and we didn't notice that we were hungry or that time was passing because the work was so stimulating.

Of particular interest in the field of NLP are the relationships between physiology (your body), your state (what you think and feel and your attitude) and your behaviour (what you do) and how changing one of these three can influence the other two.

Although the links between these three components are often unconscious, NLP has some useful techniques for utilizing these linkages under your conscious control in helpful ways.

## Using your imagination

Another important idea in NLP is about the power of our imagination. Specifically, in NLP we hold the belief that *knowledge, thought, memory and imagination are the results of sequences and combinations of representational systems. As memory and imagination have the same neurological circuits, they potentially have the same impact.* Put another way; our 'representational systems' (the pictures, sounds, smells, tastes and feelings that we experience and hold in our mind–body) are the basic building blocks of our thoughts and feelings, whether they are representing things that happened in the past or we anticipate will happen in the future.

We often talk of business leaders who are great and inspirational 'visionaries'. We also know that others have great memories and longings (or fears) for 'the way things used to be'. Our memory–

imagination is another part of the mind–body system and again NLP has some useful tools and techniques for making the most of these components to help us get the outcomes that we want. Recalling a positive experience from your memory before having a potentially difficult conversation with your boss can help to get your body and mind into a more helpful state.

## How you experience time

One additional factor that is important to our own subjective experience and is important in NLP is our perceptions of time. Like the VAKOG senses, people have preferences and experience time in different ways. Some prefer to concentrate on the future and what might be, while others prefer to focus on the past and their previous experiences. Others may prefer to concentrate more on the here and now as that is what is 'real' and present for them.

Have you noticed that people's reactions and behaviours in response to time can be different too? Some people like to methodically plan and finish tasks well before a deadline, usually to avoid the stress that they would feel if they were still working on the task close to the deadline. Others will not start the task until the deadline is very close; they might want to keep their options open until the last minute and know that they are at their best and highly energized the closer to the deadline they come.

How we represent and store time-related information in our mind–body varies from person to person too. Do you have a good memory for birthdays and other important dates? How do you distinguish between a memory that is 'real' and something that you imagined happened at a later or earlier time? If you were to point to it, where would the future be for you? In front of you, to the right or left or somewhere else?

Again, NLP has some tools and techniques that can help you understand how you experience and store time-related information and how you can usefully utilize these to get the outcomes that you want.

## ACTIVITY EXPLORING YOUR PERCEPTIONS

- How do you distinguish between something that is real and something that you imagined? How real are your dreams?

- Where is your future? Your past? Point to where they are for you in space. Where do you store your memories and dreams? How do you know where to look for them when you want to find them? If your memory was a filing cabinet, how would it be indexed?

- How strong is the mind–body link for you? How do you know when and how you experience pain, anger and hunger? How do you know if you like or dislike an experience?

## THE NLP COMMUNICATION MODEL

Have you ever wondered how it is that several people can experience the same event and have totally different perceptions of what happened? We have already touched on how we are all different and this has a bearing on how we communicate; what we prefer to receive and what we prefer to transmit when we are communicating with others.

### What is the communication model?

The NLP communication model shows us how we interpret, filter and store the vast amount of information that we receive through our five senses. It has been estimated that the eyes send at least 10 million bits of information to the brain every second, the ears 100,000, our smell sensors a further 100,000. Our touch and taste senses are also capable of providing vast quantities of information to our brain. Making sense of and storing (remembering) all that information would require a vast array of super-computers and would be enough to fill up your iPod's memory in a few seconds! All that information would just overload and overwhelm the brain if it attempted to be aware of all of it. A famous cognitive psychologist, George Miller, said that the human brain can make sense of only 7±2 chunks of information at any time; that is, between 5 and 9 chunks. The NLP communication model describes how we reduce the vast amount of data that we process and remember coming from our senses to the 7±2 chunks that we can be consciously aware of.

## Why the communication model is useful

The NLP communication model describes how we use filtering to help us interpret the sensory information we receive to make sense of the world. It helps to explain how people can view the same situation differently. You can use the model to help expand your own interpretation of events when your current understanding is muddled or causing you problems. You can use it to become more influential with others by adopting their filters and experiencing the world in the same way as them.

The filters themselves are very powerful; they modify our experience of events and situations significantly. Unfortunately, they are usually outside our awareness and act on our understanding of the world without us being conscious that they exist or the effects that they have. The NLP communication model helps us to become more aware of these filters and, with practice, to develop the ability to modify how they operate on our understanding in ways that can be helpful.

## The model

The vast amount of information that comes at us every second through our five senses would overwhelm us if we tried to make sense of it all. There are three filtering processes that modify the incoming sensory data and create within our minds our own representation of what is actually happening outside us. The filtering processes are:

- deletion;

- distortion;

- generalization.

Consequently, each one of us has our own 'map of the world': a representation or construct of how we perceive the world and the people in it. Everyone has a different map, none any more or less 'correct' or 'true' than any other and each one highly dependent on the filters we have in place.

Our perceptual filters are developed through our experience of the world from birth. Our personality, beliefs, values, language and culture are all learnt from our parents, teachers, family members, friends, peer groups, the media and the institutions we are in. When we are young we tend to make sense of the world through the explanations given to us by others. Later on we sort these out a little more by ourselves; we delete information that our filters don't recognize, we distort information that does not fit with our current understanding or personal experiences and we generalize information to fit with what we already know... and hence we create our very own maps of the world.

## The filters

### Our senses

People have a wide range of sensitivities to their five senses – sight, sound, feelings, smell and taste (VAKOG). Many people, although

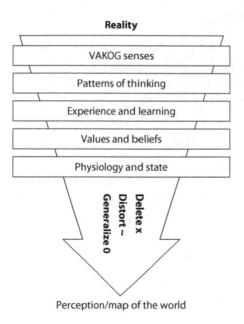

**Reality**

VAKOG senses

Patterns of thinking

Experience and learning

Values and beliefs

Physiology and state

Delete x
Distort ~
Generalize 0

Perception/map of the world

**Figure 2.3**   The NLP communication model

not all, have a preference for what they 'see'; this sense will often override or dominate the others. For other people, feelings (or smells) are more powerful at evoking a memory, state or way of thinking. In any case, we all know that sometimes we just fail to notice something even though we suspect that our senses had detected it – it simply gets filtered out. It is worth remembering that the five senses are the only way to get information from 'out there' in 'reality' into our nervous system and subsequently our perception. Often people will tell you what they have noticed and sometimes you can become aware of what they have not noticed simply by what they have or have not said. Paying attention to the sensory language that a person uses will help you identify how their sensory filters may operate.

## Patterns of thinking

These are our preferences for how we take in and process information. Each one of us will have a unique set of preferences and flexibilities in how we do this. Psychometric indicators such as MBTI categorize these individual patterns of thinking. The NLP metaprograms also act as filters which affect the way in which we perceive, understand and remember. Someone with a task focus may not notice that half the room has gone to sleep during a presentation because they are focused on delivering the speech. Someone with a similarity preference might tell you how a meeting was similar to a previous meeting.

## Experience and learning

Our memory bank of experiences, concepts, theories and understandings will affect how we notice, process and filter information too. Memories and understandings act as a reference that is used to help make sense of incoming information. Equivalences and comparisons between what we perceive and what we already know are taking place all the time and further modify incoming information so that it fits with what we expect. This is why people with a positive experience of change will welcome further change and people with a less positive experience of change will become anxious about further change.

## Values and beliefs

Our values are things that are important to us. They are 'hot buttons' that drive our behaviour. We tend to be particularly sensitive to information that either resonates with or is in conflict with our values.

Similarly, once thoughts have transformed into beliefs, they play a very significant role in governing our perceptions. Beliefs are one of the most powerful filters that help shape the maps by which we code our understanding about things. For example, a belief that people that work in a particular department, such as finance, IT, Sales or HR, behave and think in a particular way can lead us to seek evidence that confirms that belief when we encounter someone from the relevant department. In this way, beliefs can often become self-fulfilling prophecies. We tend to notice things that reinforce our own beliefs and prejudices and tend to dismiss those events that don't fit our beliefs.

### Physiology and state

How we are feeling and our physiology also play a significant role in how we perceive situations. Our biochemistry can play havoc with our perceptions. Just think about how a teenager or someone who is angry, hungover or depressed might perceive a situation differently from you. Our state, mood and attitude all act as a background set of filters that modify our perceptions. Heart rate, breathing depth, state of relaxation, tiredness and pain can all act as a further level of filtering.

## Effects of the filters

### Deletion X

We pay attention to the information that we recognize, have prior knowledge of and that fits with our previous experiences, beliefs and values. Unconsciously, most incoming information from our senses is simply ignored. If we did not perform this deletion, our information-processing system would simply overload. We have learnt to focus our attention on what is important to us and simply ignore the other distractions. As an example, there is some information that is available to you right now, but which you have probably been deleting or ignoring until you get to the next sentence. This is information about how comfortable (or not) you are, standing or sitting, the texture or feel of the chair that you are sitting in; or, perhaps, how warm or cool the room is.

You might also be able to feel the clothing that is between you and what you are sitting on. As you pay attention to those feelings, you become more consciously aware of that information and you will notice how rich and varied it is; and this is simply the feelings that you are experiencing through your backside. You might even want to adjust the way you are sitting as a result of noticing those feelings that you had previously deleted. Undoubtedly, there is a wealth of information about your team or your colleagues that you have been deleting. What do you want to pay more attention to? What do you want to look out for? If you decide that you want to become more conscious of how you feel or what is happening in the team you can consciously ask yourself what you want to pay attention to or look out for.

## Distortion ~

The importance of distortion is that it is responsible for our ability to be creative and learn through our imagination and perception. Distortion is used in creative writing, particularly when one thing is described in terms of another – ie when using a metaphor. This process allows us to bend occurrences to fit with our beliefs, our prior knowledge and experience. Distortion helps us make sense of things we might not otherwise understand, by making them fit our map of the world. Subsequently, this process can lead to a lot of communication misunderstandings when two people are referring to different maps: for example, when someone claims to think they know what another is thinking without verification, or like assuming the intentions of someone else or deeming that some action will cause something else to happen – 'If I ask my boss for clarification, then he will be frustrated at the time delay or my stupidity.'

## Generalization 0

Our beliefs are powerful generalizations that help us recognize patterns, behaviours and concepts that we are familiar with.

This process allows us to look at something or a situation and recognize it as being in the same class or category as something that we already know or have seen before. It is the major process responsible for pattern recognition, and human beings are very good at it. Generalizations are what make it easy for us to learn. We don't need to reinvent or reinterpret every situation or event that we experience; it is much simpler to compare it with what we already know to be 'true' and simply apply our learnt response. The generalization process means that we tend to miss exceptions to our reality. When we talk (or think) in 'all', 'never', 'every time', 'everyone' and 'always' language, our generalized beliefs can sometimes lead to incorrect assumptions.

## Your very own map of the world

Because we all perceive the world through our own individual set of filters, we each have our own unique map of the world. This map shapes the way we think and behave, the decisions we make and our feelings. Our maps are not the territory; they are only our best representation of the world as we experience it and given our unique filters. People operate in the world based on their own internal map; if you listen carefully to their language it will give you clues about their map and how they perceive 'reality'. And like a map, our filters can be very helpful in navigating our way through life and business. However, just like a real map, it can be helpful to ensure that the map you use is regularly reviewed for accuracy, mistakes, updates and enhancements; particularly as the environment and new meanings and understandings develop or you venture out into new territories or cultures. A review of your map can be helpful when joining a new organization or when you get a new boss. Of course, it is always helpful to remember that a map is just a map and that the map is not the territory.

# ACTIVITY  EXPLORING DIFFERENT MAPS

- The next time you listen to a presentation with someone else take a moment afterwards to discuss how you both experienced it. What are the differences in what you noticed and experienced? What do you notice about your filters and how they compare with the other person's? What can you deduce about the other person's filters? What might you do differently next time you want to communicate with them?

- Next time you make a presentation or talk to a group of people, think about how to match the audience in terms of their predominant filters. The better you are at using language that reflects the same filters as the audience, the better you will be understood. What are their beliefs, experiences and values? What is 'true' or important to them and how could you rephrase what you want to communicate so that it better fits with their map?

- Next time you feel that you are not effectively communicating with someone at work or being understood, ask them some questions about how they perceive the situation or problem, to gain a better understanding of their map. Then think about how you could tailor your communications to better match their filters. You might be surprised to find how effective matching your language to their map is when it comes to improving communications and understanding. What questions would you ask to help you explore someone's map of the world?

# SUMMARY

- Human beings are 'creatures of habit'. We put effort into learning new abilities and then, with practice, the ability can be performed unconsciously. Similarly, breaking an unhelpful habit requires awareness, practice and effort.

- Our five senses are the only ways that we can get information into our perception, understanding and memory. Becoming more aware of this raw sensory information and our own preferences for what we notice is a helpful first step in any learning process.

- We have two basic modes of motivation: 'Away from' thinking which is driven by fear and stimulates our flight-or-fight response, and 'towards' thinking which utilizes our imagination and is usually longer lasting and less stressful than 'away-from' thinking.

- Gaining an awareness and appreciation of our motivation can be helpful. NLP values 'towards' thinking very highly, which helps us to think more in terms of our desired outcomes rather than focusing on the problems that we are experiencing or what we don't want to have happen.

- We all have different preferred ways of processing the information that we receive through our senses. Gaining an awareness of our own personal preferences for these thinking patterns and recognizing those preferences in others can help make communication and understanding more effective.

- NLP acknowledges that there are links between your physiology (your body), your state (what you think and feel and your attitude) and your behaviour (what you do). Developing a conscious awareness of these elements and how they are linked can help you to make the changes that you desire to each of them.

- The NLP communication model describes how we naturally, and usually unconsciously, filter all of our available sensory information down to an amount of information which we can comfortably make sense of. Filters include our preferences for rep system, thinking patterns, our beliefs and values, our experience and learning and our physiology and state. These filters all act on the sensory data by deleting, distorting and generalizing. As a result of this filtering, we each build up our own unique map of the world.

# MANAGING YOURSELF

**Knowing yourself is the beginning of all wisdom.**
ARISTOTLE

Being able to manage yourself generally gives you confidence and credibility when you start managing other people. Having self-awareness is a fundamental prerequisite to being able to develop yourself further. If you don't know where you are starting from or where you are going, how will you know when you have got there? Being aware of yourself includes understanding how you do things, how you make sense of the world and how you choose to interact with the world. In many ways, you need to be able to manage yourself effectively before you try to manage anyone else. This chapter provides the tools and ideas to support you in developing a greater awareness of yourself and the impact you have on others.

Have you ever had an experience where the reaction you got from someone was different to what you had expected, perhaps taking you by surprise? This may have been because you were not paying sufficient attention to how the other person was responding to you. Developing your ability to notice what is happening around you, paying attention and becoming more aware of what is happening within you in any given situation can help reduce the likelihood of your having experiences like this.

If you have not been getting the results you expect, it can be helpful to become more aware of your own habits and routines and to explore how well these work for you. It may be that the routines or approaches that worked in one context don't work in other situations. This is often the case where people have been promoted or changed roles and have not developed new ways of doing things that reflect the new responsibilities they now have. Although the routines worked in the old job, they don't work in the new job. This requires us to develop new skills, routines and flexibility in our thinking and behaviour to help us operate in new ways in the new context. This helps us to have more choice about how we respond and therefore to be more effective.

If we want to achieve success in life and work, it is helpful to have an idea of what we want to achieve or to specifically identify in what way we want to be fulfilled. Identifying our goals and dreams and being able to turn these into well-thought-through plans rather than vague aspirations can make a significant difference to our chances of achieving our ambitions.

Have you ever felt that life was not fair and that your life was affected by the behaviours and attitudes of others? How helpful or useful was this? Developing a willingness to take personal responsibility for your feelings and actions and to learn how to manage your state so that it is helpful and useful to you in achieving your objectives can make a significant difference to your life and work. Being able to choose how you want to feel can be very liberating and can help to reduce the effects of other people's moods and attitudes on how you feel and your own effectiveness.

NLP techniques and approaches to address all of these issues are covered in this chapter.

# ENABLING AND LIMITING BELIEFS AND THE NLP PRESUPPOSITIONS

People make business decisions based on their beliefs and assumptions, usually without being consciously aware of their underlying beliefs. They do this when they are making an investment, deciding whether to hire someone or whether to discontinue a product or service; they are working within the framework of their beliefs and assumptions. In order to make good decisions and to understand what is important to us, it is helpful to be aware of our own beliefs and assumptions. This is particularly important if our beliefs are getting in the way of our success and we want to change them or if they are working really well for us and we want to reinforce them.

## What are beliefs?

Our beliefs are a set of rules that we take to be 'true': rules about ourselves, other people and how the world works. Our beliefs are usually a generalization about relationships or meaning. We are not born with beliefs. We learn our beliefs. They develop over time as we entertain thoughts, build up our store of experiences and notice patterns. What you believe has a profound effect on how you behave and how you experience the world through your perceptions.

## Why are beliefs important?

> Whether you believe you can, or you believe you can't, you're right.
> HENRY FORD

If you believe that a merger is going to be successful you will tend to look for the evidence of this and work towards this outcome. If you believe that it will fail you will tend to focus your attention and energy on the evidence of it failing and may even inadvertently contribute to it failing.

Once our thoughts have transformed into beliefs, they play a very significant role in governing our perceptions. They are one of the most powerful filters that help shape the maps by which we code our meanings about what we perceive. As perceptual filters, we tend to be highly attentive to noticing when our beliefs are confirmed. This describes how we endow beliefs with a self-fulfilling quality. Existing beliefs can prevent a person from considering new evidence or a new belief.

Rather than concerning ourselves with the truthfulness or falseness of any particular belief, NLP categorizes beliefs as either enabling or limiting in any particular context or situation. If you believe that 'most people are trustworthy' then you are likely to trust people when you first meet them. However, if you believe that 'most people are deceitful' then you are likely to be suspicious when meeting new people. These two beliefs have very different impacts on the way that you behave when you meet someone for the first time. In the context of meeting new clients, customers or colleagues and making a good impression, one belief is enabling and the other is more likely to be limiting.

## Conducting a belief audit

We all have beliefs that we have formed from our experiences over time. Some beliefs are enabling and help us achieve our outcomes and others are limiting and hold us back from achieving our outcomes. Often we are not aware of our beliefs until we are challenged or challenge ourselves to review our own map of the world. This can happen in response to feedback or when we recognize that we are not achieving our outcomes. We can all change our beliefs if we want to. After all, most adults no longer believe in the tooth fairy or that the moon is made of cheese.

You would be amazed how some beliefs that individuals have held for many years continue to act powerfully and unhelpfully for them simply because they have remained unchallenged. 'You can't teach an old dog new tricks' and 'Better the devil you know than the devil you don't' can be extremely limiting beliefs to hold in some situations where a more constructive or positive outcome is desired.

Once you become aware of a belief it is helpful to ask yourself:

- Is this always true? What are the consequences if it is always true?

- What else has to be true to support this belief?

- What would be a more enabling belief in this context? What has to happen for that enabling belief to be true in this case?

## The NLP presuppositions

The study of successful communicators by Bandler and Grinder when they first developed NLP, elicited the following enabling beliefs, which are known as the 'NLP presuppositions'.

1  The map is not the territory.

2  The meaning of communication is the response you get.

3  There is no failure, only feedback.

4  Present behaviour represents the very best choice available to that person at that precise time.

5  Every behaviour has a positive intention.

6  Mind and body are part of the same system and anything that occurs in one part of the system will affect the other part.

7  The person with the most flexibility in thinking and behaviour has the most influence in any interaction.

8  Choice is better than no choice.

9  If one person can do something, then anyone can learn how to do it.

10  Everyone already has everything that they need to achieve what they want.

11  A person's behaviour is not who they are.

12  Language represents internal experience.

13  It is not possible to not communicate.

14  There is a solution to every problem.

15  Resistance in another person is a sign of lack of rapport.

16  Knowledge, thought, memory and imagination are the results of sequences and combinations of representational systems. As memory and imagination have the same neurological circuits, they potentially have the same impact.

These enabling beliefs can be helpful and useful in supporting you to achieve your outcomes. It is not necessary to wholeheartedly believe that the presupposition is true in all situations or contexts (although you might believe it to be so). It is only necessary to act as if it was true. For example, if it is true, and *there is a solution to every problem*, would you be more motivated to continue working on a problem until you found a solution than if you were still entertaining the limiting belief that some problems have no solutions?

Examining your beliefs or taking on a presupposition, even if it is just on an 'act as if' basis can be very helpful when you want to try a different approach or you are feeling stuck. I keep a copy of the presuppositions in my top drawer and when I get stuck with a problem or I'm not achieving my outcome, I can generally find a presupposition to help me shift my thinking.

All the above NLP presuppositions appear in other chapters of this book. We have marked them *like this* so that you can easily find them and be aware of the sorts of situations and contexts in which they can be powerfully enabling.

Mike was anxious about presenting his report to the Board. He hadn't met the members of the Board before and his boss had told him that they could be very robust with those presenting reports, if they felt that they were being misled or not given the full picture.

Mike had spent a long time drafting his report and covering all the possible angles the Board might challenge him on. Despite this preparation he was still anxious about presenting the report.

He asked his boss for advice who agreed that it was important to be prepared and that it was important for the Board to feel confident about the proposal. They would ask questions to ensure that the proposal was realistic and Mike's job was to answer their questions so that they could make a decision. They were not interested in 'making Mike look small' (the limiting belief that was making Mike anxious), they wanted Mike to help them make the right decision. Holding the belief that it was his job 'to help them make a good decision' was much more enabling and helpful for Mike.

When he presented his report and was asked questions, Mike was able to respond confidently without feeling that the Board members were challenging him personally. The Board felt able to make a decision based on the recommendations in Mike's report because he had been confident and helpful in his responses to their questions.

# ACTIVITY TRYING ON SOME ENABLING BELIEFS

- Practise 'trying on' different beliefs. Pick one and hold it to be true for the duration of the exercise. What else has to be true while you hold that belief? How does it affect how you perceive the situation? What do you notice?

- Review the list of NLP presuppositions and identify which of them are already true for you and which are not. Which of them would be helpful or useful to you, if they were true? When? Now consider what might happen in that situation if you acted as if it were true. What would you do differently? How might that affect the outcome?

- Some of the presuppositions might be completely untrue for you – almost objectionably false. That's fine. Develop an awareness of your own beliefs and consider what they give you. There are likely to be some helpful and unhelpful implications of holding any belief to be true in all situations.

- You could spend some time reflecting on your own beliefs and considering which of them are helpful and which of them are unhelpful in supporting you to achieve your outcomes. You could then refine your own beliefs so that they are more helpful or useful to you in each context.

- How have you changed your beliefs in the past? What process did you follow to change that belief? Could you use that method again to change any limiting beliefs you have identified into more enabling ones?

- All of the quotes at the beginning of each chapter of this book are beliefs. Try them on and notice what happens when holding those beliefs. How might they change how you think, feel or act in a given situation? Are they enabling or limiting in that context?

# IMPROVING YOUR SENSORY ACUITY

The range of what we think and do is limited by what
we fail to notice.
RONALD DAVID LAING

Have you ever discussed your experience of a meeting with a colleague who was in the meeting and realized that their experience was different from yours? One of my colleagues is very good at picking up how people are feeling and she will often comment on this. I am much more aware of what people are doing or saying. Sometimes she misses this information in the same way that I miss information about how people are feeling. It can be useful to be aware of what you pick up on and what you miss.

## What is sensory acuity?

Sensory acuity is how much and what you notice from your five VAKOG senses: sight, sound, touch, taste and smell. It is amazing how much information we sense but don't really pay attention to. Take a moment to listen to all of the sounds around you, right now. You were probably not aware of these sounds until you directed your attention to focus on them. The same will be true for what you can see, feel, smell and taste.

## Why is improving your sensory acuity helpful?

By spending some real effort to see, hear and feel more of what is actually happening around you, you can greatly increase your personal effectiveness. The wider the range of information you pay attention to, the more likely you are to get a fuller sense of what is going on. This can be helpful in achieving your outcomes. Sensory acuity is a form of feedback which will tell you whether you need to keep doing more of the same or whether an adjustment is necessary. Noticing this kind of information requires a state of curiosity: to really find out what is going on here.

Often we are focused on what we want to say and on getting our message across, and are not sufficiently focused on how our message is being received by the other person. By paying attention to both yourself and the other person in any interaction you can gain additional information, which can inform the choices that you make about the way that you are communicating. The greater your sensory acuity, the more likely you are to be able to read the response signals you get from the person you are interacting with. Imagine how helpful this might be in a work context. Once you can do this well you will be able to detect when your message is not being received as you intended and then you can decide whether you want to ask questions to check what is happening for the other person or you can simply adjust your message or the way that you are delivering your message.

## Developing your sensory acuity

To develop your sensory acuity, first get curious about yourself. Start to notice what you notice:

- What do you notice?
- What do you not notice?
- What often gets deleted for you?
- What have you not noticed before?
- What do you notice in yourself?
- How are you feeling right now?
- What do you notice about your own feelings or your current state?
- How does this change as you respond to experiences during your day?
- What signals are you giving out through your body language, tone of voice and the language that you are using?

Now get curious about others and start noticing what you notice about other people:

- What do you notice about them?

- What does that movement mean?

- Why did they use that phrase?

- What does their sensory language tell you about their VAK preferences?

- What did you notice about their tone?

- Putting it all together, what is your overall sense of this person?

Remember that this is additional information that you are seeking to make sense of from your world. If the information is what you have noticed about another person you may want to ask them about this to check out your assumptions (eg 'I notice that you are tapping your pencil on the table, and I am wondering what that tells me about how you are feeling or what you are thinking?').

## ACTIVITY  PRACTISE NOTICING

- What if, the next time you were in a conversation with someone, you paid attention to how they were responding to you, maybe by asking yourself the above questions?

- To further develop your sensory acuity, the next time you go for a walk you could choose to concentrate on a single sense. If you wanted to further develop your visual acuity you could focus on what you can see, the number of different colours, different shades, the light and the shadows, the detail of your surroundings or the patterns. Spend some time noticing information from your least preferred VAK sense. What do you notice now?

- Our sensory preferences are evident in our language. You could analyse your own language to identify your sensory preferences, either by recording a conversation and playing it back or reviewing something that you have written.
- Becoming curious about information that you have previously not noticed (by unconsciously deleting it) is a great way to develop your sensory acuity. Where will you start to notice those really useful things that will make a big difference to you getting your outcomes?

# DEVELOPING YOUR OWN FLEXIBILITY

## What is flexibility?

> It is not the strongest of the species that survive, nor the most intelligent, but the ones most responsive to change.
> CHARLES DARWIN

In an ever-changing world the ability to adapt and be flexible is a key skill to ensure not only our survival but also our success and resilience. The more flexibility we have the more choices we have. The more choices we have the more likely we are to find an approach that works. In the ever-changing world of business our flexibility can make the difference between business success and failure.

## Why is developing flexibility so important?

A person's physical flexibility refers to their ability to move their joints and muscles through a full range of motion. Improving physical flexibility allows an individual to perform activities more effectively, enhance their performance and prevent injury. The same is true of mental and emotional flexibility: the greater our flexibility in thinking and behaviour, the wider the range of choices and responses available to us in a given situation. Remember that old proverb from the previous chapter, the one that says 'If you always do what you have always done, then you will always get what you always got.' If what you are doing is resulting in getting the outcome that you want, then fine – continue to do just that. However, if you are not getting your desired outcome, then developing some flexibility and adapting to what is happening outside you and trying different approaches to problems and issues are likely to be more effective than doggedly sticking to what you have always done. Taking a different approach to solving problems or adopting a different way of thinking about a problem will often lead to new insights and breakthroughs. The NLP presupposition is that *the person with the most flexibility in thinking and behaviour has the most influence in any situation*.

Often we can fall into our preferred ways of doing things or of thinking about things. We sometimes refer to these as routines or habits and they are often done unconsciously. Sometimes these can work really well for us and at other times they can limit our understanding and reduce the number of options or apparent choices that we believe are available to us. Having the flexibility to think differently about a situation or to take a different perspective or point of view can be helpful in providing new insights and choices. And we already know that *choice is better than no choice*. In today's business world, conditions change rapidly. Therefore the more flexibility you have, the more choices you have in a given situation.

## ACTIVITY  HOW TO DEVELOP YOUR OWN FLEXIBILITY

Developing flexibility can be achieved with practice with the desire to expand our own range of responses:

- Take a moment to put this book down and fold your arms.
- Now unfold them and fold them differently – the opposite way around.
- Notice how this feels.

Typical responses to this exercise can be that this feels strange, awkward or uncomfortable, and that you have to really think about it. This is the difference between our usual, preferred way of doing things and a new way of doing things. To develop flexibility takes practice and initially there will probably be a sense that the new approach feels strange or requires more effort. You might become very conscious of your incompetence at doing something differently the first time you try it.

You can develop your flexibility by being curious, by trying new things and by having an open mind. Choosing to see situations from a number of different perspectives can help to increase your flexibility too. Actively listening to other people's points of view without judging these can help you understand and appreciate different approaches and ways of doing things. Moving from thinking there is a right and wrong way to thinking that there are numerous ways of achieving something increases your flexibility and helps prevent you from becoming stuck in your ways.

Utilizing your flexibility requires you to have noticed that your habitual way of doing something is no longer achieving the results or outcome you desire. This is where your sensory acuity helps you to identify that a different approach may help you achieve your outcome more effectively.

There might be many times in business when you get frustrated that you are not getting the results that you want. It can be really helpful to take a moment to stop and consider what other choices you have which could achieve your results. The trick is to notice that what you are doing is not getting you your desired results and to have the flexibility to explore alternative options.

# ACTIVITY PUTTING YOUR NEW-FOUND FLEXIBILITY INTO PRACTICE

- The next time you experience a situation that you would like to be different or the next time you want a more appealing outcome, how could you choose to think about it differently?

- What aspects of your usual routine of noticing, having feelings, thinking and behaviours would you like to change? Changing which of these would have the most positive effect on your outcome? Alternatively, you could challenge yourself to try something new on a regular basis.

- You could review a problem or issue that you have and rather than ask yourself how it is similar to problems that you have encountered in the past, instead focus on what is different about it.

- If you know someone who is very good at doing what you need to do, you could ask yourself how they might approach the issue. What might they do differently from you? What would it take for you to adopt their approach rather than your usual routine?

# WELL-FORMED OUTCOMES

**A goal without a date is just a dream.**
MILTON H ERICKSON

Why is it that some people achieve great things and others don't? Some people seem to have a very clear vision of where they are going; they may call it their ambition or their dream and they seem to make steady progress towards achieving that ambition, whilst other people may have dreams but they don't translate them into reality. Sometimes people put this down to luck – you are either lucky or unlucky. Interestingly, very few successful people put their success down to luck. Most put it down to spotting and utilizing opportunities which move them closer to their goals. It can be helpful to understand what the people who make progress towards achieving their ambitions do, so that you can use the same techniques. We have already seen that being very clear about your outcome using 'towards thinking' helps you achieve that outcome.

## What is a well-formed outcome?

A well-formed outcome is one that has been explored and checked for a number of aspects that will help to improve the likelihood of achieving that outcome. This NLP methodology provides a checklist of things to consider when developing an outcome and helps you identify what needs to be in place to increase the chances of you achieving that outcome. This technique is helpful when setting business goals. It provides a process to thoroughly examine the goal and understand the upside and downside of achieving it. It also helps to establish how the goal will be achieved and what personal resources are required to ensure delivery of the desired outcome.

## When would it be useful to consider the well-formedness of an outcome?

Applying some rigour to the outcomes you have ensures that you have considered all the factors that will enable their success and any barriers that may prevent them. Having a good towards-thinking outcome is a really great start and by exploring thoroughly all the factors which contribute to the achievement of the outcome, you are in a better place to ensure these are addressed and the outcome is achieved.

This technique can be applied to work-related projects and the development and delivery of corporate strategies and visions as well as personal goals. The method works equally well for yourself or with a team that share a common outcome.

# A checklist for outcome well-formedness

Any outcome is achieved within a system of interlinked elements. As you make changes to one element in the system, the other elements will be affected. This is an iterative process for analysing and making adjustments to those various elements that might affect your outcome. There are a number of checklist items to consider, and you should feel free to revisit the outcome itself as well as the previous checklist items as many times as necessary to achieve an outcome that is not only desirable but also coherent and in congruence with all the elements of the system.

## Stated in positive terms

We already know that a towards-based motivation can be a longer lasting, more powerful and more pleasant way of motivating oneself than doing so with an away-from outcome. It is important that your outcome is stated in positive terms to get the full benefits of the neurological processes that will make it happen. The outcome should state what you do want to happen and not what you want to avoid happening. Choosing the words of your outcome, and writing them down, in a positive frame is the first step in the process. An example would be 'to maintain or grow our market share' rather than 'avoid our market share shrinking further'.

## Initiated and maintained by self

> I wanted to change the world. But I have found that the only thing one can be sure of changing is oneself.
> ALDOUS HUXLEY

Make sure that the outcome is something that is within your or your team's control; something that you can do and maintain. If the outcome is not something that is self-maintainable by you or your team, then you will need to restate it so that it is. It needs to be something that is not reliant on others. Changing others directly lies outside our control; changing them indirectly by changing ourselves is something that we can do. Rather than 'Get my colleague to complete his tasks on time more often', a well-formed version would be 'For me to develop my motivation, persuasion and project-review skills sufficiently that my colleague is more willing, able and likely to complete his tasks on time'. It can also be helpful at this point to consider and write down what is really important to you about achieving the outcome. This can be done by answering the question: 'What will achieving this outcome give me, the team or the organization?' An example of something that you can do and maintain as a team is to review and relaunch your marketing strategy or improve the quality of your services. Whereas, hoping that the competitors lose market share through poor service or quality is not something you can deliver.

## Sensory-specific evidence for achievement of outcome

The next step is to imagine a sensory-rich 'target' for the outcome. This will help to make your goal more compelling. It can be helpful to act as if you have achieved the outcome. Daydream a little and go there. For example:

- What are you noticing now that you have achieved your outcome?

- What do you see, hear and feel?

- What is it specifically that tells you that you have achieved your outcome? What is the evidence?

Doing this as a team can help to ensure that everyone in the team has a shared understanding of the outcome and will be able to track whether progress is being made towards the achievement of that outcome. Each individual might provide their own piece of specific sensory information that forms part of the overall team vision. This process gives your mind a reference point for the desired outcome and helps you to recognize the evidence you will be seeing, hearing and feeling that indicates you are making progress towards your outcome. As a team you might explore what your outcome is like and you could develop a metaphor for those attributes of success that represent the team's outcome. This can serve as shorthand for what you want to achieve as a team.

## Context

Make your desired outcome appropriately contextualized:

- What is the context in which this outcome will be achieved?
- What, where, when and with whom?
- Set a realistic timeframe.
- What is included and what is not? Where are the edges or boundaries?
- What steps are required to reach the desired outcome?

### ACTIVITY  DEVELOPING A WELL-FORMED OUTCOME

Think about your current business circumstances. Now, assume that you have achieved your outcome and as a team you are looking back from that achievement. Notice what is different. How have you got to this outcome? Who has been involved? What was the timescale? What were the key steps? How did you manage your stakeholders? Whose support made all the difference? What were the barriers and the enablers? How long did it take? What were the surprise discoveries along the way? You can have great fun, letting your imagination run wild here and you will find that it helps smoke out key areas you need to pay attention to.

## Ecology

The next step is to check the ecology of your outcome. Ecology is the study of consequences of making a change in a system: in other words, considering how any change that you make impacts on the wider system of which you are a part. The principle of ecology is very important in NLP. Ecological considerations are what differentiate ethical and authentic use of the NLP tools and techniques from those that are more manipulative and self-serving. An ecological check means stepping back from the proposed change to think about it in a disassociated way. It will also involve thinking about the change from the point of view of others in the system. (These changes in perspective are known as perceptual positions; we will explore them fully in the next chapter.) Evaluate the impact of the outcome to see if there are likely to be any unintended consequences that might be negative, harmful or unnecessarily expensive. Doing this gives us an opportunity to debug and refine the change before it is implemented. Questions to consider at this stage include:

- For what purpose do you want this? What are the intended effects of this change?

- Does this change address the present problem, or something else?

- Does this change increase the availability of choice? Will it take away any currently available choices? For you and for others?

- What will you gain and what will you lose when you have achieved this? By achieving the outcome do you lose or disrupt something else?

- How does this change affect others that are part of the system? What do they lose? Is this acceptable to you and is it representative of who you are (your values) and who you want to be?

- What other effects might this change have, and are those effects desirable?

- Is this outcome still a good idea? What needs to happen to make the outcome ecological?

## Identify the resources required

Successfully achieving your outcome will require that you have access to appropriate resources necessary to make the change. 'Resources' here refers to the NLP concept of resources as personal qualities like determination, focus or confidence, although it is a good idea to consider other resources here too:

- What are the internal resources (personal qualities) that you need to achieve your outcome?

- Are these up to you and are they maintained by you?

- Which resources do you already have and which do you need to acquire?

- When have you had these resources in the past?

- Other resources: what physical assets or objects are required to achieve this outcome? What other people, skills or know-how? What is the budget?

## Desirability

Given all those searching questions about your outcome and all that analysis, is this still something that you want?

- Do you still want this outcome?

- On a scale of 1 to 10, how desirable is it now?

- If it is less than a 7 or 8, what could you do to make it more desirable?

- What needs to happen to make it even more compelling?

Outcomes that are not sufficiently desirable are unlikely to gain the commitment necessary to make them happen. Sometimes, going through the well-formed-outcome process will help people realize that what they thought they wanted is not actually worthwhile or that desirable after all. This can save them all the effort of embarking on a change process that is unlikely to achieve the originally desired outcome. On the other hand, the process is very good at highlighting any additional benefits of achieving the outcome that might not have been previously considered. It even gets the participants to experience all those benefits when they go to the outcome and act as if it has already happened. In such cases the desirability can increase to a level that propels those involved to take the first step.

## First step

> A journey of a thousand miles begins with one step.
> LAO TSU

Commitment comes from taking the first step, not thinking about it!

- What is the first step, which you'll take within the next 24 hours, to achieve this outcome?
- What specifically will you do? What will you see, hear and feel yourself doing?
- Imagine yourself taking that step.
- And now make a commitment to yourself to take that first step.

## ACTIVITY  PUTTING THE PROCESS INTO PRACTICE

What if you used this NLP technique to develop your business plan or to identify how you were going to achieve a particular business goal? This technique can be used for big strategic ambitions as well as small or incremental business outcomes. Having worked through this process, your mind has created the conditions for you to achieve your outcome. You are now prepared, and will be able to make the most of opportunities that present themselves because you have developed your sensory acuity to spot opportunities as they arise; and you have developed your flexibility to make the most of those opportunities, to achieve your well-formed outcome.

# STATE MANAGEMENT: CHOOSING YOUR ATTITUDE

Men are disturbed not by things,
but by the views that they take of them.
EPICTETUS, ANCIENT GREEK PHILOSOPHER

You can probably think of a time at work when you have felt resourceful; a time when you have felt confident in your ability and capacity to tackle a problem or rise to a challenge or overcome an obstacle. Equally, I suspect that you can also recall times where you have felt unresourceful; times where the answer has seemed elusive, where the problem has felt intractable and where you seemed to be going round in circles. Both examples reflect different states of resourcefulness and it can be helpful to be able to access the appropriate internal resources when you need them.

## What are resources and anchors?

In NLP, a resource is some personal quality like confidence, focus or calm which, if available to you, can help you to achieve a particular outcome. A resourceful state is a state of being in which the appropriate helpful resources are readily available to you.

Anchoring is a good way of getting yourself into a resourceful state of mind that supports you in the way that you want to feel, how you think and how you want to be in order to achieve a particular outcome or goal.

## When are anchored resources important?

Confidence, clarity, focus, calm and curiosity are all states of being that are helpful in certain situations, especially in a work context. What would it be like if you could choose which state you wanted for a particular situation and turn on that state 'at the touch of a button'?

You might already have noticed that different people react to situations in different ways. While some might get angry or frustrated about something, others will be able to simply shrug it off or even find the very same situation amusing. What would it be like if you could choose how you felt about a situation based on the reaction that you thought would give you the best chance of getting what you wanted out of the situation rather than just relying on your usual, automatic and unconscious response? How helpful would that be at work? Imagine if you could shift your response from an energy-sapping reaction to an energy-enhancing reaction.

## What states do you have anchored already?

Have you ever had an experience and found that the memory of that experience comes back to you every now and then? It might come back to you if you hear a particular sound or piece of music. A picture might trigger the state. A particular smell might take you right back to a time when you first became aware of that aroma, and you relive that first experience. Have you noticed when this happens you get the same feelings that you had when the situation happened the first time? Sometimes you get these feelings even more intensely than when you experienced them the first time. These memories can have an impact on the way you do things today. You will have wonderful memories of great times that you treasure and these may even have been at work!

Anchoring a state is a natural process that usually occurs outside of our awareness. Does the name Ivan Pavlov ring any bells for you? He was a behavioural psychologist who did some famous experiments that involved ringing a bell before feeding some dogs. Soon the dogs associated the sound of the bell with the arrival of food and would start to salivate. Pavlov called these 'conditioned reflexes' and in NLP we would call the sound of the bell the anchor that triggers the salivating state. You can use anchors to allow experiences to be available to you consciously, utilizing the natural process that we usually use unconsciously.

## ACTIVITY MEMORY

Take a moment to think about a happy or positive memory and notice what happens to your feelings and your body. Your mind recreates the sensations you have stored in your memory that are connected or anchored to that experience.

For example, when you were young you probably took part in activities that gave you great pleasure. The pleasure was associated with the activity itself, so when you think of an activity or are reminded of it, you tend to re-experience some pleasurable feelings. You can use this natural phenomenon to actively manage your state. The more sensory specific you make the memory, the more vividly you will relive it and the feelings associated with it.

You may also have had bad experiences that can stop you from doing things; even things that you want to do. Being able to manage your state can help you overcome barriers, phobias and limiting resources that may be unhelpful to you. It can also help you call up helpful resources whenever you need them and when they would be most useful to you. The NLP presupposition that *mind and body are part of the same system and anything that occurs in one part of the system will affect the other* is an important belief to hold to be true here.

Understanding that we can have a choice about our mood, state of mind and energy levels can be a key moment of realization for many people. Understanding that we are in control of our mind and our body means that we can more easily become conscious of what happens to us in particular situations. If we are in a bad mood, an unresourceful state of mind or have low energy levels it is because we have (unconsciously) chosen to be in that state. It can be quite challenging to recognize that we make choices about our mood and our state of mind. It means that there is no one else to blame for how we feel. This can be a revelation for some people.

## Changing your state 'on demand'

We have all developed routines, habits and strategies for what we need to do in life. These can include our strategy for getting to the office on time, or our approach to meetings or problem solving or how we deal with other people. Many of our strategies work well for us and have stood the test of time; others may no longer work so well for us and may need to be revised.

Mostly, our strategies are deep in our unconscious and we are not aware of them. These strategies are often reflected in our preferences and our patterns of thinking. Our strategies are like computer programs that run automatically for us in a given situation. These programs are written when we learn things for the first time. They are reinforced when we repeat these behaviours and thinking and they govern our actions or reactions in certain situations.

Like Pavlov's dogs, we humans also program ourselves to have certain responses to certain stimuli. Our stimulus–response programs can be very helpful; for example, when your alarm goes off in the morning, you wake up. These programs can also be unhelpful, such as when someone arrives late for a meeting and you get irritated or when a mobile phone goes off during your presentation, you get angry. If you want to change these responses to ones that are more helpful or useful, you can.

## How to switch state to a more resourceful one

Between stimulus and response there is a space.
In that space is our power to choose our response.
In our response lies our growth and our freedom.
VIKTOR FRANKL

Becoming conscious of your programs can be the first step to changing them. Our reactions to a stimulus can feel instantaneous and so automatic that they don't seem to be a choice. When asked about this, individuals will often say 'I had to' or 'it was the only option'. A presupposition in NLP is that *choice is better than no choice*. Knowing that you have a choice about your state at any moment in time can be very enabling, allowing you to consciously choose a different state if your current state is not working for you at that particular moment. By exploring alternative responses to a stimulus we can create alternative options that may be more helpful or useful to us in the future.

When we notice the trigger or stimulus that switches on the unhelpful state, we can explore how to create a gap between that stimulus and the response (the unhelpful state) which allows us space to consciously choose a more helpful response from a range of alternative responses.

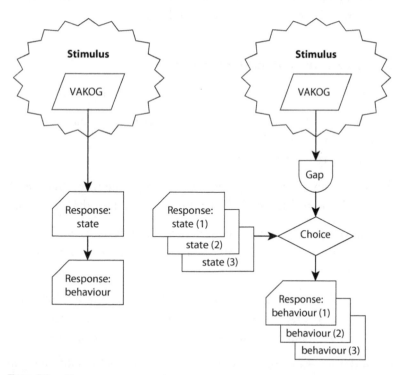

**Figure 3.1**   Choose your attitude

## An example of a helpful state change

A salesman who drives for a living was getting increasingly frustrated by inconsiderate drivers who would cause him to have to brake suddenly and those who drove very cautiously and held him up. He was reacting badly, driving too close, flashing his lights and blowing his horn when these situations occurred. He was arriving at his destination stressed and angry and as a result his sales figures were falling. He worked with a coach to explore what alternative responses he could develop for these situations. Now, whenever he notices that the car in front is too close, sees brake lights come on or has that feeling that he is going to be late, he pulls back and gives the car in front plenty of space and laughs at its leisurely pace. Now he arrives at his sales meetings relaxed and fully focused on the sale and feeling much more in control of his state. His sales figures are now much better.

## Steps to a more resourceful state

1  Identify an ineffective response that you habitually have.

2  Identify the trigger that stimulates your habitual response. What do you see, hear and feel immediately before you start your current, automatic response?

3  Identify an alternative response that might be more helpful or useful in that situation. What state is required for that response?

4  Can you recall a time when you have previously had that state? What did you see, hear and feel then? What are your anchors for that state?

5  Using the anchors that you have for that resourceful state, imagine yourself holding that state and responding to the situation. What happens? Was it a more useful response?

6  Find a state and response that you think or feel would give you a better chance of getting the outcome that you want. Make

any necessary changes and mentally rehearse the situation until you are happy with the outcome. This useful technique of mentally rehearsing and testing a new state and behaviour before putting it into practice is known as 'future pacing'.

7  Now put it all together and imagine the stimulus (the trigger) in all its sensory vividness, the anchor that invokes the resourceful state, and then see, hear and feel yourself doing your more helpful response.

8  Now think of something completely different. Break the resourceful state that you invoked with the anchor in the previous step. What did you have for breakfast last Saturday? Now repeat steps 7 and 8 several times over.

9  Next time you experience the trigger, you will know that you have a choice about how you respond.

## How will you use state management?

The next time you find yourself reacting to a situation in an unhelp-ful way, you can now take a moment to reflect on the range of alternative responses you have available to you. Having rehearsed each option you will find that the next time the stimulus happens you will create a gap to allow you to make a conscious choice about your response. Of course the original response remains one of the options available to you; however, you now have more control over your responses and can actively choose a response that is more helpful or useful to you.

Having this skill means that when you review a situation or experience you can identify which strategies worked well for you and which worked less well and need to be changed now to ensure better outcomes in the future.

The process of anchoring and accessing resourceful states is used extensively in the world of sport. Many athletes develop a gesture or adopt a certain posture or movement, which is their anchor for a resourceful state and helps them perform at their best. When the time comes to play the shot, take the penalty or start the race, they will trigger their anchor to recall and access this resourceful state. You might find it helpful to anchor your resourceful state with a similar gesture or movement. Use a gesture or movement that is unique and appropriate for deploying at work. Increasingly, business leaders are using these techniques to anchor the resourceful state they want to have when making a presentation or giving a live interview on radio or television or when meeting with suppliers or customers.

## ACTIVITY ANCHORING

Next time you are feeling particularly resourceful and it's an attitude or state that you think you might find useful again in the future, anchor it there and then. Notice what you see, hear and feel and make a mental note of all the things that you sense that are associated with that state. You might want to think of a gesture, movement or posture that you will use as a kinaesthetic anchor for that state as well – adopt that physical anchor there and then too. Then, when you want to call upon and access that state again in the future, you will have a rich and vivid set of VAK memories that you can use as an anchor to access it.

## SUMMARY

- Our beliefs are a set of 'rules' that we use to make generalizations about relationships and meaning. Rather than categorizing beliefs as either true or false, in NLP, we recognize that many of the beliefs that we hold are based on and affect our perceptions. Consequently, they might be more usefully categorized as 'enabling' or 'limiting'.

- As our beliefs have such a powerful effect on our perceptions, it can be helpful to develop the ability to hold more enabling assumptions in certain situations – giving us more choice about how we feel or react.

- NLP has a list of useful presuppositions. These are all 'enabling' beliefs that have been held by, and have been modelled from, people who have exhibited remarkable communication abilities. Choosing to adopt these enabling assumptions can be helpful in certain situations.

- Developing our sensory acuity, the ability to notice information from our senses that we would usually and unconsciously delete, distort or generalize, is a useful skill to develop when looking at a situation that we are finding difficult. Doing so can often provide additional and enlightening information that helps us understand the situation better and potentially find a solution.

- Developing flexibility in our assumptions, sensory acuity and our preferred thinking and behaving patterns can help us manage difficult situations more effectively. By shifting our usual perceptual filters and habitual behaviours we can operate more usefully in a wider range of situations and we can interact more effectively with others' maps of the world.

- Building on our ability to think imaginatively about the outcomes that we want to achieve, and visualizing those outcomes, can be a more effective way of working out 'how' to tackle a problem, than starting with thinking about how to move away from the problem itself. The well-formed-outcome process is a set of steps to help you plan what you will have needed to do to reach your outcome, working from your desired end result backwards.

- Recognizing that we have generally developed habits in the way that we respond to certain situations can be a helpful first step if we want to respond in different, more effective ways. Gaining an awareness of the 'anchors' that usually, and unconsciously, trigger unhelpful states and behaviours can help us identify these events and give us choice in how we respond. Particularly, when we have practised and mentally rehearsed thinking, feeling and behaving in those new ways in response to that trigger.

# MANAGING OTHERS

Having developed some tools and techniques that have enabled you to better understand yourself, you are now in a good position to consider how you might extend their effectiveness to help you manage and influence other people to achieve their outcomes, your outcomes and those of your organization.

In NLP it is recognized that everyone is unique and has a different experience of the world. That means that the people you are responsible for managing will be different from you in their patterns of thinking, in the way that they experience the world, in what they believe and value and probably in many of their desired outcomes.

This requires you to have the flexibility to adapt to these differences and to manage each person in the way that delivers the best outcomes for that individual, your team and the organization.

Being able to build rapport and connect with your people is helpful in enabling you to understand what is important to them, for you to be able to communicate effectively with them and to appreciate what motivates them and makes them tick. You need to be able to step into their shoes to be able to really access their map of the world and what is true for them.

# BUILDING RAPPORT

There will be some people that you work with, with whom you naturally have great rapport. There will be others to whom you find it more difficult to connect and who sometimes might feel like hard work. The chances are that you have more in common with those you get on with than with those you find difficult. When we have shared values, experiences and thinking patterns, building rapport seems very natural. However, when there are different values, experiences and thinking patterns it may be more challenging to connect and build rapport; we may need to work at this to make our communication more effective and to achieve mutual understanding.

## What is rapport?

Rapport is one of the most important features or characteristics of unconscious human interaction. It is a commonality of perspective, of being 'in sync' or being on the same 'wavelength' as the person with whom you are talking. It is the quality of harmony, recognition and mutual acceptance that exists between people when they are at ease with one another and where communication is occurring easily. You can tell when a couple are in rapport because their body language matches and they mirror each other's movements and gestures and use each other's words and phrases. Have you ever watched a couple having a meal in a restaurant? You will see them lift their glasses and drink simultaneously and their movements are often synchronized, and they do all of this unconsciously.

## Why being able to build rapport is useful

In general, we gravitate towards people that we consider similar to us, because people like people who are like themselves. In rapport, the common ground or similarities are emphasized and the differences are well understood, respected and minimized. Rapport is an essential basis for successful communication. It is helpful to consider that any *resistance in another person is a sign of lack of rapport.* Once you have built rapport with someone, any initial resistance will simply dissolve away. Trust and mutual respect will increase. Your communications will be more effective: both what you hear and what you say. You will better understand each other and be in a better position to manage, persuade, influence, sell to and negotiate with each other. The ability to do this is very helpful in a business context, particularly if you are working with people from a different culture or business sector where there might be different values, beliefs and expectations of how you interact at work.

## How to build rapport

Many people unconsciously create rapport by matching the person that they are talking to. To further develop this ability it is necessary to become conscious of your own matching skills so that, with practice, you can move to even greater levels of rapport. Effective ways of creating rapport are by subtly matching both verbal and non-verbal communication, especially voice patterns, body language and eye-contact patterns and by developing a genuine interest in the other person and in their model or map of the world. Becoming curious about the other person's map of the world and asking them some open questions is a good way to start this process. Subtle body-language mirroring is another useful way to begin. Do as little as is necessary to achieve rapport, since it must be subtle enough to be out of the other person's conscious awareness:

*Step 1.*   Match the other person by subtly matching their non-verbal behaviour. Use your curiosity to build a genuine interest in their model or map of the world.

*Step 2.*   Pace or test the level of rapport that you have with the other person by making a small non-matching change in your own non-verbal behaviour. If they follow, which usually happens 20–60 seconds later with a similar shift, then you have rapport. If not, go back and repeat step 1.

*Step 3.*   Once you have adequately paced the other person for a time, you can start to lead. Think about your outcome. What are you trying to achieve? This means a slight change of direction and very often of energy level too. You can test (pace) this leading carefully and if you get a negative or non-reaction, go back to match for a while before you try pacing and leading again. In NLP this technique is known as match–pace–lead (see Figure 4.1). Leading or being directive will often be met with resistance unless there is sufficient rapport. Matching is the way to build that rapport and it can be tested by pacing.

To extend your ability to create rapport, you need to have excellent sensory acuity and flexibility. Spend time practising just one form of matching until you can use this easily and without thinking about it. Then add another element, then another, and so on. That is all there is to it: keen observation and practice. With consistent practice you will be able to effortlessly create rapport with total strangers in just a few minutes, whether or not you like them, and whether or not you have existing areas of common interest. Remember that engaging in rapport must be subtle. If the process intrudes into the other person's conscious awareness they may respond unfavourably and become uncomfortable. You may know someone at work who is very good at building rapport. You can notice what they do and then try this yourself. Like any skill development, planning, practice and then reflection help to develop the skill so that it becomes more natural.

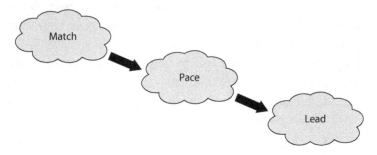

**Figure 4.1** Building rapport

## ACTIVITY PRACTISING YOUR RAPPORT-BUILDING SKILLS

You could practise these skills by focusing, for the first part of any interaction with someone else, purely on building rapport.

What if you could develop a conscious awareness of the level of rapport you have with others at any time? Could you learn to calibrate the level of rapport and know whether it is at a sufficient level to generate great communication?

Can you build rapport with conscious effort until these skills become unconscious?

You can use the same skills in reverse to break rapport when you need to. This means that you have the skills to manage your communications and not get stuck talking to the most boring person in the office or at a party. Mismatching, when you are too deep in rapport, is a good way to focus attention on getting a decision. It can also help if you feel that you are overly influencing the other person and they are just agreeing with you to be polite or because you are their manager.

Some people find the idea of matching another person to build rapport rather uncomfortable or 'false'. They feel they might be trying to fool or take advantage of the other person. To help overcome this uneasiness, it is important to remember that matching is a natural process that usually takes place unconsciously. Second, as you already know, being really clear about what your outcome is can be very helpful. If your outcome when building rapport is to improve your understanding of the other person's map of the world and enable more effective communication to take place between you, would that make some conscious matching more acceptable to you?

In business, we need to be able to work with a wide range of people, some of whom we may not otherwise choose to spend time with. In these circumstances, it can be really helpful to focus on the benefits of investing some effort in building rapport with those people in order to achieve your business outcomes more easily and effectively. This is essential if the person happens to be your boss or someone that you manage!

# FRAMING AND REFRAMING

The pessimist sees difficulty in every opportunity.
The optimist sees the opportunity in every difficulty.
WINSTON CHURCHILL

Being able to see a different point of view or perspective in business helps you to find your way around problems and constraints. It is an important skill in managing others, particularly when it is helpful for them to see things differently or have a different perspective on a situation.

## What is framing?

Framing is how we make sense of something and structure our experience. One person can see a glass as half full and another can see it as half empty. Both are right and yet which is the most helpful and useful way of seeing the glass? Of course, this depends on the context. For example, if I'm at a party I might look at my glass and think 'It's half empty already – I had better slow down my drinking if I'm going to get any work done tomorrow.' On the other hand, I might think 'It's half full – I've still got half a glass of wine to enjoy.' To reframe something is to change its meaning by putting it in a different setting, context or frame.

A business example would be a company manager announcing that 'We've lost a major contract' and then saying 'Another way of looking at this is that we now have time to research and explore expanding into an adjacent market with higher margins.'

## When can reframing be helpful?

How we choose to frame a situation or an experience depends on many factors and influences. We have a tendency to frame situations without thinking consciously about them. This feels natural because it is habitual. If the way that you frame situations or experiences works for you that is great. If it is not working for you then it is helpful to think about what alternatives you have to frame things differently in a way which is more helpful for you and your team.

Recognizing that you have an element of choice about how you frame your experience means that you are one step closer to making choices that are most helpful and useful to you and the people that you manage. It can be helpful to consider, what is the most useful way to frame a situation, given the outcome that you want to achieve? This will guide your choice about how you frame the situation. When people have a similar frame of reference, they are likely to be able to understand each other quickly, as they start from a similar place.

Being able to frame a situation in a particular way can be helpful in influencing others. If you need to motivate a demoralized team you are more likely to be able to influence them if you first acknowledge that they have had a tough time (matching and pacing) before you reframe their view towards the future when things are likely to get better, rather than simply jumping in and saying 'Come on, guys, get to it...'.

Framing a difficult situation as a 'disaster' will probably not be as helpful as framing it as a 'learning opportunity'. While a 'disaster' frame may disable people and prevent them from looking forward, a 'learning-opportunity' frame may open them up to exploring a more useful attitude to the situation. You have already seen the NLP presupposition that *there is no failure, only feedback*. This can be a very helpful reframe in similar situations. What would it be like if you could choose the best frame for the outcome that you want in any difficult situation?

## How to reframe

Simply restating a comment with a different frame can sometimes be very effective. An example of this might be: 'We didn't get agreement at the meeting', which could be reframed as 'We have another opportunity to work on our arguments and persuade people individually before the next meeting.' Reframing in this way is most effective when you have built some rapport with the other person first. So remember to match and pace them before you start to lead with your reframing statement; remember also that *resistance in another person is a sign of lack of rapport.*

Another, more subtle, way to reframe is by asking a question that will help the other person to do the reframing themselves: 'What else does this mean?' or 'What is another way of looking at this?' This will help them to see that they have choices about which frame they use for a particular situation. Jokes and humour are often very effective reframes and the humour can help to make the shift in frame more easily accepted. Put another way, humour can reduce a person's resistance to thinking about something in a completely different way. However, care is needed with humour, to ensure that the joke results in a more useful or helpful frame rather than one that is cynical or sarcastic.

## ACTIVITY  PUTTING REFRAMING INTO PRACTICE

- How could you reframe some of your own assumptions and beliefs in a way that is more helpful for you and moves you closer to your outcome?

- Start to notice the sorts of frames that your colleagues use. Do you notice any patterns or favourite frames that are frequently used and unhelpful? What opportunities do you have to reframe these?

- Sometimes a reframe that works well for you will not work with someone else. It is all about the different maps of the world that we have. Find a reframe that works in the recipient's map of the world and remember that any reframe requires a level of rapport to be effective; otherwise it's just spin.

- If you are someone who already has the ability to use humour to reframe situations, consider how you could utilize this skill to get even more effective and useful reframes, ones that move you and others more quickly to their outcomes.

## PERCEPTUAL POSITIONS

Being able to step into someone else's shoes is a very helpful technique for gaining a better understanding of what is going on for them in a particular situation. This can help you get an insight into why they are behaving as they are particularly if they are not behaving as you would expect.

## What are perceptual positions?

Perceptual positions are the NLP technique that allows you to gain insight into a situation or interaction between people by looking at the situation from three completely different perspectives. This can be incredibly useful in a work context, for example, when you have had a discussion with someone and they have not reacted in the way that you expected.

## CASE STUDY

Jane was asked by her line manager, Carlos, for an update on a project she was running. She became angry and asked her boss why he didn't trust her, to which her boss replied that he did trust her. She replied: 'You obviously don't.' This was behaviour that was out of character for Jane and her line manager was confused and a little offended.

A little later Carlos reflected on the exchange and reviewed what had been happening for him (first position). He had lost track of progress on the project and wanted a quick update. He realized that he was also a bit embarrassed that he had lost track of things.

When Carlos stepped into Jane's position (second position), he took on her body language and thought about what was happening in her world. Her body language made him feel tense and he recalled that she had previously told him that she hated being chased for project updates and that it made her feel like she was being nagged and that she wasn't trusted. What was important to her was to

▶

anticipate when updates were required and to provide these without being asked. Upon stepping into her shoes, Carlos realized that she may have been upset that he had asked for an update.

Then he thought about this interaction from a third perspective; one taken from outside their discussion looking in at the two of them. When he did this, he noticed that Jane seemed to pride herself in doing a good job and that he had asked for an update on a project ahead of the scheduled update. It became clear to Carlos, when he took this third position that he needed to apologize to Jane and explain that he had lost touch with the project rather than Jane having failed to do provide a scheduled update.

## When might using perceptual positions be helpful?

By understanding things from more than one perspective, we can increase insight, options, flexibility and choices about future actions. This is useful if you want to reflect on an exchange which you feel didn't go as well as you would have liked.

## Using perceptual positions

There are three positions in the perceptual position technique. These are shown in Figure 4.2.

### First position: the 'I' position

In this position, state the situation from your own perspective or point of view and from your own map of the world or reality. Actually feel the experience and fully associate into it. Now give yourself some self-advice from this position. What could you do differently?

**First position:** seeing the world from your own position. 'What's important to **you**?' Experience how you feel and think about the situation (associated).

 **Second position:** seeing the world from their position. 'What's important to **them**?' Experience how they feel about the situation (associated).

**Third position:** seeing the world **from outside** the situation. As an independent observer, ask 'What is happening here?' Dissociated – analytical and without emotion.

**Figure 4.2**   Perceptual positions

## Second position: the 'you' position

In this position you process the situation from the perspective of the other person and take into account how the experience would be from the other person's map of the world. You see, hear and feel the situation from their position. Really step into it. Imagine their beliefs, values, feelings and thinking, and fully associate with their reality. Use everything that you know about this person to help you do this. This is easier if you stand in a different space from the one you used for the first position and it can be helpful to take on the same posture, movements, language and voice tone of the other person. Be careful not to 'contaminate' the second position with your own first-position judgements. You need to leave yourself and your map of the world behind at the first position to do this cleanly. To help you leave any personal judgements that you have out of the second position, it can be helpful to hold the belief that *present behaviour represents the best choice available to that person at that precise time and every behaviour has a positive intention*. Next, state the situation from this position. How do 'you' see things when you are in second position? Now, give some advice from this second position; what would 'you' like to have happen?

### Third position: the 'they' position

Move to an uninvolved, dissociated, analytical position and report on the situation from the 'outside'. Imagine yourself as a BBC World Service reporter watching the situation play out from a balcony where you can clearly see the events and situation. This is the position that people take when they take 'the helicopter view'. Consider what is going on here and describe from that dissociated perspective what is happening. Give some logical and unattached advice from this position. Unlike the first and second position, the third 'they' position is emotionally detached and comments are only on specific observable facts.

### Bringing it all together

Next, stand back in the first position and become yourself again. What do you notice? Given what you have heard from the second and third positions, what advice would you give yourself, here in first position? What have you learnt? What will you do differently in the future? This technique allows you to gain an insight into another person's world and what is important for them in a given situation.

### Developing your perceptual flexibility

Notice that the first and second positions are both associated and the third position is dissociated. Association is when you step into a situation and fully connect to the experience. Dissociation is when you step outside the situation and take a detached view of things. Like other patterns of thinking, we each have our own preferences around whether we unconsciously choose to experience a situation in an associated or a dissociated way. And like the other patterns of thinking, it can be useful to develop some flexibility and conscious choice over which pattern we adopt at any time. Similarly, people often have favourite perceptual positions from which they prefer to operate. Getting stuck in any of the three perceptual positions has the following effects:

- stuck in first position – you might become egotistical;

- stuck in second position – you might become a rescuer or caretaker;

- stuck in third position – you might become cold and unfeeling.

## ACTIVITY PUTTING PERCEPTUAL POSITIONS INTO PRACTICE

- Next time you have a difference of opinion with some-one or they react in a way that you didn't expect, take a moment to consider the situation from the three perceptual positions.

- The technique is best learnt with another person acting as 'coach': helping you move between the three positions cleanly and pointing out when there is any 'contamina-tion' from another position. Once you have practised the process a few times with a coach you will be able to move more easily and cleanly between the three positions on your own.

- Which is your preferred position, the one that you most naturally and unconsciously take when situations get difficult? Which is your least visited position? What does moving to your least favourite position give you?

- How much practice moving between first, second and third position (whilst reflecting on past interactions) do you need before you can move quickly and gracefully between all three positions, in real time, whilst engaging with someone?

# MOTIVATING OTHERS

Tell me and I'll forget; show me and I may remember;
involve me and I'll understand.
CONFUCIUS

Being able to motivate others is an important management skill and one which you will need to be able to deploy in most work situations, whether you are managing a team to deliver a business goal or you are encouraging colleagues to deliver something that your team needs to achieve its outcomes.

## What is motivation?

Motivating another person is to cause that person to act or to stimulate their interest in an activity. It is a way of focusing their attention and engaging their energy to achieve a specific outcome.

## Would being able to motivate others be useful for you?

Managers are expected to be able to motivate their people to achieve the organization's objectives. Managing self-motivated people can be great as long as their outcomes align with the business. Managing people with low levels of motivation can be more demanding. The most important tool in these circumstances is clarity regarding a compelling and well-formed outcome. Once you have this and can describe what you will see, hear and feel when the outcome is achieved, you will have a tool that will entice those who have a preference for towards thinking. For those with a preference for away-from thinking, you might need a different approach. They are more likely to be motivated by how the outcome will help them avoid the risks and potential hazards that concern them. Doing this will support them in moving towards the outcome. You may also find it helpful to reframe 'away-from' concerns or issues so that they are more 'towards' focused with questions like, 'And so what would you like to have happen instead?'

## How to motivate people

The most effective way of motivating others is to understand them and to know what makes them tick. Being aware of their aspirations, goals and objectives will enable you to hook into these when you are seeking to persuade them to invest their energy, thoughts and actions in delivering the organization's objectives. If you know what it is that they want to achieve, you can present whatever it is you need doing in a way that also meets their outcome. You need to use your flexibility and imagination to do this well.

Two simple ways of motivating people are to either sell the benefits of doing what needs to be done or to threaten them with the consequences of not doing what needs to be done. This is known as the 'carrot-or-stick' approach. In some ways the stick approach can work well, particularly in the short term. If you want to maintain motivation over an extended period, the carrot approach tends to be more effective and is usually a more pleasant way to be motivated too.

To really understand what will motivate someone to work harder or deliver more, you need to understand what is important to them. One way to do this is by using the perceptual positions technique and stepping into their shoes to really appreciate the world from their perspective (second position). Alternatively, you could explore with them their map of the world, using your curiosity and some open questions. Once you have an understanding of what is important to them, you can adapt your style to match what they want.

Using perceptual positions and building rapport while utilizing your own curiosity and flexibility, you can gain considerable insight into, and understanding of, other people's maps of the world. You can use this understanding to shape your style and approach to best match the individuals or teams that you are motivating. Remember, you don't have to agree with their view of the world or their beliefs and values; you simply need to recognize and acknowledge them in order to build rapport and to influence them towards achieving the required outcomes.

## ACTIVITY BECOMING AN INSPIRATIONAL LEADER

- Given what you already know about your direct-line reports, identify whether the carrot or the stick is likely to be most effective in motivating the team into action.

- What are your own preferences for motivating yourself? It is likely that you will naturally adopt a motivating style with others that you have unconsciously been using to motivate yourself. Does your preferred style always serve you well? Does it best match the needs of those that you manage?

- What styles of motivation work well in your organization?

Management hierarchies, levels of expertise, rank and sometimes simply job titles can create a culture where away-from or stick motivation styles become the norm. This style can come unstuck when organizations need to become more adaptable, flexible or creative, or need to work with partners that don't share the same values, or need to reorganize into a matrix style of management. Away-from styles are also less effective when motivating upwards (your boss) and sideways. Developing some effective towards motivational styles and techniques can be very helpful in these cases.

You now have a number of additional approaches and techniques to practise and deploy at work when managing others. With practice you will now be able to:

1 build rapport with anyone;

2 reframe their perceptions so that they are more helpful and useful to the people you manage;

3 step into the shoes of your people and better understand how they experience the world;

4 appreciate what motivates you;

5 understand whether your team members are motivated by what they do want to happen, or by what they don't want to happen.

## SUMMARY

- Rapport is the natural and usually completely unconscious process that we follow when we build a connection, understanding and relationships with others. It can be helpful to gain a conscious awareness of this process so that you can choose how and when to utilize it most effectively. Leading others towards an outcome is much more effective if you have first matched and paced their state, body language, thoughts and feelings.

- Not only do we filter the information that we receive through our senses to build our map of the world, we also consider that information within certain frames of reference. By developing some flexibility and adjusting the frame of reference that we use to consider the information, we can sometimes see things in new and enlightening ways. Outcome thinking is just one example of how we might reframe a 'problem' situation.

- In NLP, the frames of reference – your own perspective (first position), the other person's perspective (second position) and the perspective of an emotionally detached observer (third position) – have special significance. Practising and developing the ability to move swiftly and gracefully between these different perspectives, in real time, can help make your interactions with others much more effective.

- Developing the ability to step into the shoes of others and understand their perspective on a situation (second position) is a fundamental step in motivating them. The ability to match them in this way will help you decide the most effective way to pace and then lead them to the outcome which you or they want to move towards.

**5**

# POWERFUL USE OF LANGUAGE

If you speak to a man in a language he understands,
you speak to his mind; if you speak to a man in his
own language, you speak to his heart.
NELSON MANDELA

## THE POWER OF LANGUAGE

In business we are all interested in getting our message across as effectively as possible. Being able to influence and persuade others is helpful whether you are managing them, selling to them or being managed. How well we communicate with others determines how successful we are. Go into many organizations and you will hear people complaining that 'the problem round here is communication'. It is often the first thing to be blamed when things go wrong.

This chapter sets out how you can communicate clearly and specifically with people and how you can clarify your understanding of what others say to you. It also explains how you can enhance your communication by using certain words instead of others and how you can engage people and motivate them by using artfully vague language. We also cover the way that we communicate unconsciously via our body language, and the importance of ensuring that our body language and tone match the words that we are using to convey our message. Humans are very good at picking up incongruence between body language, tone and words. Often we will do this at an unconscious level. By becoming more conscious about how we communicate, you can increase your range of communication methods and have more chance of getting your message across and securing your outcome. Now doesn't that sound good?

## Being specific: the meta-model

Have you noticed how often people speak in generalizations or non-specific language at work. Statements like, 'No one listens around here' or 'It's always the same' or 'They don't understand how hard we work' are uttered in offices every day. Sometimes it can be helpful to question these statements to understand what is really being said and also to establish what the speaker wants to happen instead.

## What is the meta-model?

The meta-model is a set of questioning techniques that can enlighten and help understanding, both for the person asking the questions and the person being asked. The meta-model was developed by Bandler and Grinder in the very early days of NLP, between 1973 and 1975. They carefully studied the language patterns used by therapists who were very good at effecting positive change in their clients. The meta-model is a set of quetions that seek to challenge the distortions, clarify the generalizations and recover the deletions made as people speak about a particular issue.

## When is it useful to use the meta-model?

We have seen in the communication model that people have to filter the information that they get from their senses in order to make sense of what they experience. The filters that we use distort, delete and generalize the information from our senses to make our own internal representation of what is happening on the outside, in 'reality'. Without these filters we would simply be overwhelmed by the vast quantity of information available to us. People build up their own map of the world based on the rules that they implement for activating these filters. When we speak, our language will reflect the distortions, deletions and generalizations that we have implemented to make our own map. *Our language represents our internal experience*. When we communicate with someone else, it is helpful to remember that they will have a different set of filtering rules from ours. The meta-model is a useful way of understanding how these filters are operating, both for ourselves and others involved in the communication. Meta-model questioning can help you understand what is going on for another person and how they structure their experience. Understanding that can help you to identify how that person's map of the world is different from your own. When you modify your language so that it better fits with others' maps of the world, you will have more rapport, be better understood and be more persuasive. It can be helpful to remember that *the meaning of communication is the response you get*, rather than what you meant it to mean. Furthermore, meta-model questions can be used when you adopt a coaching style of management. They can be used to help someone find their own solutions to their problems, rather than burdening you with the responsibility of fixing the problem for them.

# Asking open questions at the meta-level

There are two types of questions that you can ask: open questions and closed questions. Closed questions can be answered with a single word or phrase, often a simple 'yes' or 'no'. Open questions, on the other hand, usually elicit a longer answer. Closed questions usually refer back to the questioner's map of the world, whereas open questions invite the respondent to think and reflect, and to give their feelings and opinions based on their own experience and map. Open questions hand control of the conversation back to the respondent.

Closed questions are great for starting and ending conversations and summarizing progress. However, they do little to get the other person really thinking or give you any useful information about them and their own map of the world.

Bandler and Grinder found that the effective therapists did not ask many questions about the content of what their clients were saying but instead asked lots of questions about the structure of what they heard. It was as if they were taking a higher-level or 'meta' view of what was being said. Asking questions at this meta-level seemed to unlock, illuminate and clarify many of their clients' issues – more so than asking questions about the content of what was said or making directive statements about what needed to change. The effective therapists approached each client with the belief that *everyone already has everything that they need to achieve what they want.* The clients were the experts in the content of what they experienced and that did not need to be challenged. The therapists simply needed to help the clients become aware of the structure of their experience.

You can follow a meta-model style of questioning by following these simple steps:

1 Build some rapport with the other person.

2 Become curious about the other person's map of the world. Put your own map of the world out of reach – in this context it can only cause you to make invalid assumptions.

3 Listen carefully to what the other person is saying.

4 Notice the structure of the statements that you are hearing rather than getting involved in the details of the content.

5 Be curious about what the other person is saying. If it helps, furrow your brow a little, turn your head to one side and adopt a curious tone of voice when you ask your open questions.

6 Ask an open question ('How...?', 'What's important about...?', 'Describe...?', 'Where...?', 'When...?' or similar) about the structure of what you have heard to recover or 'undo' the deletions, distortions or generalizations.

Overuse of meta-model questions can sometimes seem challenging to the other person, so make sure that you maintain rapport by using some statements and closed questions to summarize whenever you feel it appropriate.

## Some examples of meta-model questioning

*'She's a much better candidate.'* A comparison has been made by the speaker but not stated. 'Much better than whom?' or 'Better in what respect?' would help to recover the deleted comparison.

*'People treat me as if my contribution is not valued in this company.'* 'Who specifically treats you as if your contribution is not valued?' would recover who these undefined 'people' are. 'How do you know that they think that?' or 'What specifically do you see, hear or feel tells you that?' will further enlighten the generalization and potential distortion embedded in the original statement.

*'My manager is really annoyed with me.'* This is an example of 'mind reading', a form of distortion filter. An appropriate meta-model question would be 'How do you know that your manager is really annoyed with you?' or 'What tells

you that your manager is really annoyed with you?' A useful follow-up meta-model question would be 'And what else could that sort of response from your manager mean?'

'*You are always questioning me about my work. You don't trust me.*' This is an example of another type of distortion: attributing meaning to something or thinking that it is linked to or equivalent to something else. In this example the speaker has a rule that says that asking questions about their work means that (and can only mean that) they are not trusted. A suitable meta-model question would be 'What else could my asking questions about your work mean?' or 'Can you recall asking a question of someone that you trusted about their work?'

'*They never listen to me.*' The word 'never' in this statement tells us that a generalization has been made. Other such words are 'always', 'every', 'no one', etc. An appropriate meta-model response to a generalization is to take the word that the person has used and simply reflect it as the question. In this case, 'Never?'

'*We are not communicating well here.*' In this statement much of the useful information about the communication has been lost. 'How, specifically, would you like to communicate here?' might well recover some of the information that has been filtered out.

'*You just can't do that sort of thing in this organization.*' Statements such as 'must', 'should', 'shouldn't', 'won't', 'can't', 'need to' are all generalizations that reflect a rule-bound map of the world that can limit people's behaviour in helpful and unhelpful ways. The above could be challenged with 'What would happen if you did?' 'According to whom?' or even 'What would have to happen to allow that sort of thing in this organization?' In all cases you challenge the speaker to find their own counter-examples for the rule rather than suggesting your own.

*'We expect you to behave in a professional manner.'* 'Professional' in this sentence is a generalization – like the 'communicating' example above. To recover the lost information you could ask 'How specifically do you expect me to behave?' or 'What specifically would you see, hear and feel when people behave in a professional manner?' Asking for the sensory-specific information in this way can be particularly helpful when asking meta-model questions about behaviour.

## ACTIVITY PUTTING META-MODEL QUESTIONING INTO PRACTICE

- Start to notice how many questions you ask compared with statements that you make in particular situations. Then start to notice how often you currently use open and closed questions. Sometimes people are reluctant to ask open questions as they feel that it will hand control of the conversation over to the other person or seem like they don't understand what is being said. However, people usually feel more listened to and better understood when they are asked open questions. What does it take for you to feel comfortable enough to ask more open questions?

- Practise focusing on the structure of what someone is saying rather than just the content. What has to be true for them to say that? What rules are they applying? What have they deleted, distorted or generalized in order to make that statement? Sometimes it can be easier to practise this with written statements. 'Agony aunt' columns in newspapers and magazines are a great source of material to practise your meta-model questioning style. You can also review e-mails from a particular person. The same deletions, distortions and generalizations will show up in their conversations. You can do your homework by reviewing their e-mails and then be more alert to what they tend to delete, generalize or distort from their own map of the world.

- How could you encourage someone else to start asking you more open rather than closed questions (which are really just statements about their own map of the world)? How would it feel to be asked more open questions? And what would that give you?

# PERSUASIVE LANGUAGE

I'm sure you would like to be able to use persuasive language at work wouldn't you? What if you could learn to influence and persuade your colleagues much more effectively? Would that make work a much more fulfilling experience for you?

## What is persuasive language?

Have you noticed that some people seem to 'talk a good talk' or are very persuasive, influential and even charismatic, while others induce feelings of boredom or worse? Some specific words and language patterns can be more powerful than others, in both positive and negative ways. So it's useful for you to be able to become skilful in noticing and using language in the most effective ways that you can.

## English grammar and being persuasive

Grammar defines a set of rules about how language should be structured and used in a technically 'correct' way, particularly the written word. However, using correct grammar **does not** always make your communication more effective, more persuasive or more influential. Sometimes breaking written grammar rules when you speak can help to make what you say more effective.

## Using sensory-specific language

Sensory-specific language is very powerful for engaging others simply because it stimulates our basic sense of what we experience rather than requiring the cognitive effort to process, which more abstract talk requires: 'How does that grab you?', 'Do you see what I mean?', 'Does that ring any bells for you?' compared with 'Are you fully understanding the meaning of what I am trying to convey?'

Technical training such as engineering, science, the law and accounting often encourage the trained 'experts' to both write and speak at a high level of abstraction far removed from sensory-specific language. Such people often talk in concepts and theories and use jargon and acronyms that are far removed from our everyday sensory experience. Unless you are communicating with someone who has had the same technical training as you, then think about how you can use more sensory-specific language to effectively get your point across.

As with all communication, noticing and reflecting back the other person's preferences will help to ensure that they pay even more attention to you. So if you are communicating with someone who uses lots of visual language (they will also probably look upwards when speaking if they have a visual preference), then talking in pictures about how you see the situation is likely to be more effective than talking about what you hear or how you feel about it. When communicating with a large audience, it's helpful to ensure that you use a wide variation of visual, auditory and kinaesthetic language rather than just using your own preference. This will help ensure that you connect with everyone in the room.

## Some powerful words

### 'And' and 'but'

The word 'but' masquerades as a simple conjunction – a word that simply joins two phrases or clauses. However, it has a sledge-hammer effect on whatever was said before 'but'. Read the following two sentences and consider the efforts of today compared with future efforts:

> 'We have done a lot of work today but there is still a lot of work to do.'

> 'We have done a lot of work today and there is still a lot of work to do.'

For most people 'but' greatly diminishes or even deletes the phrase that preceded it. Once you know this you will find that in most cases it is more effective to use 'and' instead. Consider the brutality of 'I understand your point but...' compared with the less confrontational 'I understand your point and...'. Of course, once you are aware of the power of 'but' you can use it purposely to diminish one clause and then focus the listener's attention on what follows. For example: 'I'm sorry things have not gone the way you wanted them to but think about what you have learnt.'

It is usually considered bad grammar to start a written sentence with 'And'. However, 'and' is so effective at joining two phrases together – seamlessly – that it can be very effective when used to start your answer to a statement made by someone else. 'And' allows your statement or question to exist simultaneously with what they have said, even if it contradicts what they have said.

Furthermore, using 'And' at the beginning of your statements can help to maintain rapport with the other person, even if you are disagreeing with them. This additional rapport will mean that what you are saying is likely to be met with less resistance. For example, notice the effect in the following exchange:

> *'I don't want to chair the budget meeting again tomorrow if Finance are going to be there!'*

> *'And think about what you achieved yesterday when you did chair the meeting, that you could put that to good effect again tomorrow, if you did decide to chair it again.'*

The 'And' in the reply acknowledges and accepts the first statement, including the 'don't want' part, while offering an alternative view. The leading 'And' helps to soften the counter-proposal and makes it more likely to be accepted than the same reply without the leading 'And'. Of course, replacing the 'And' with a 'But' is likely to significantly increase the resistance put up by the first speaker and is likely to seriously diminish the level of rapport. And by using 'and' rather than 'but' at work you will start to notice the difference this makes to maintaining rapport with your colleagues and your ability to persuade and influence them.

## 'Why'

'Why' is traditionally included in the list of words that make great open questions – together with 'how', 'what', 'where', 'when' and 'who'. However, you will probably have noticed that 'why' often puts the other person into a defensive position and forces them to provide a justification rather than a more candid or objective answer. This is particularly true if you need to probe deeper and ask the 'why' question more than once. A good alternative to 'why' is 'And what's important about...?' For example, if someone says 'I really don't want to present this report at the meeting tomorrow', then a reply such as 'Why?' or worse still 'Why not?' is likely to put them on the defensive and provide a justification for their stance and might even push them to a more entrenched position. In contrast, a 'And what's important about not presenting tomorrow?'

is likely to demonstrate that you really want to understand the reasons and elicit a more informative response.

## 'Try'

'Try' is a word that seeks or gives permission to fail. Whenever you 'try' to do something rather than just doing it, you set an expectation that you will not succeed. You set this expectation for both yourself and the listener. The same thing happens if you ask someone else to 'try' to do something. Your request comes with an embedded command that they won't be able to. If you hear someone else say that they will try to do something, ask them what it would take to just do it? It will help them consider and focus on the thing that will enable them to do it. This can be the difference that makes the difference. And now you can start to notice when people say 'try' and you now have a choice about whether to encourage them to just do it.

## 'Do' and 'don't'

We have already seen that the brain needs to make a representation of the thing that you want it to move towards or away from, and how compelling that representation can become. Remember the 'Don't think about Elvis' exercise where Elvis kept appearing? It is more effective to motivate yourself and others by building a representation of the thing that you do want rather than the thing that you don't. It gives the brain a positive reference of what it needs to move towards that the brain will keep checking for.

Often people can get very stuck thinking about what they don't want to happen and, like the Elvis exercise, they often end up with what they don't want as the result. The question 'And what do you want to have happen?' can help people switch out of the away-from thinking mode and imagine a representation of what they do want instead. Furthermore, asking them what they would see, hear and feel when they achieve what they want will help them to build a compelling representation of that 'do want' with visual, auditory and kinaesthetic parts. This technique utilizes the powerful motivation provided by our imagination. Interestingly, this technique is used by many hypnotherapists to help people create a representation of themselves as slim, confident, healthy, happy non-smokers rather than the things that they don't want to be; talking in terms of 'do want' rather than 'don't want' works well without having the other person go into a deep trance. This also works well with a team when setting targets and plans for the future. If the team has a shared sense of what they want, including the specific evidence, they are in a better position to achieve their targets and plans, as they have a clear and compelling 'target' that they can focus their attention and energy on as they move towards it.

## Time language

### *Future*

Talking about the future or using the future tense can be helpful to get others to imagine possibilities. Sometimes people can get very stuck in their present problems and by asking 'What will it be like when...?' or 'What would you like to have happen instead?' will direct their attention towards future possibilities. As we have seen before, asking a question in this way is often more effective than telling someone where to focus their attention or what to do, and is usually met with less resistance than something like 'You ought to consider...' or 'If I were you...'. These are statements from the questioner's map of the world and can feel as though they are imposed on the individual creating resistance. Although they can be very well meant they don't engage the individual's map of the world. Open questions such as 'What will it be like?' require the individual to engage with their own map of the world to answer the question. The answer they come up with is much more likely to be compelling because it comes from their own map of the world and is owned by the individual themself.

## 'Now'

The word 'now' is very effective at directing the listener's attention to the here and now, and their own participation in it. This can be helpful when the immediacy or urgency of a situation needs to be emphasized or when a decision needs to be made. For someone who is stuck in reliving a past situation or lost in the number of future options or possibilities open to them, a question such as 'What do you need now?' can help them to focus on the present and take some immediate action. 'Now' can also be useful to bring the attention of team members to the present moment. After debating an issue in a team meeting, the team leader might say, 'And now that we have aired our views we need to decide what we are going to do next'.

## Past

Talking about the past will help people to relive those past experiences and memories. Just watch them go back in time when you mention 'how things used to be' or ask them to tell you what happened in a particular situation. When you do this the person will often re-experience the whole situation including the emotions associated with those past memories (feelings, pictures, films, sounds, etc). Depending on the situation that you direct them to, you can bring about good feelings and memories (nostalgia) if you want them to feel good about what they want to move towards in the future or you can induce less happy memories and feelings if you want to remind them of what they need to move away from.

## Mixing up time

Once you have mastered the techniques set out above you can mix up different tenses in the same sentence, which can merge past, present and future together, giving a sense of continuity. For some people this might cause an element of confusion; which in turn can help lead to openness to new ideas and ways of thinking:

'And as you are looking back now, you will have noticed how much has already changed in this organization so soon, then, now, hasn't it?'

'Now, then, remember how good you will feel this evening about how well you perform later today.'

## Being artfully vague

As you will recall, the meta-model involves asking open questions about the structure of what a person is saying in order to recover what has been deleted, distorted or generalized in their map of the world. There is another model in NLP (the Milton model) that does the exact opposite of the meta-model and transforms language into less specific phrases that the listener has to add their own meaning to in order to make sense of it. This can be effective when giving a speech to a large audience or communicating with an individual or team in an engaging or charismatic way. It is a linguistic technique used widely, both consciously and unconsciously, by performers, politicians, leaders and inspirers.

Using abstract or general words and phrases (rather than being specific) often leads to a higher level of rapport with the listener. They will need to add some specific detail to the vague language in order to make sense of it for themselves. When the language is artfully vague, the listener finds the missing specifics from their own map of the world and adds those to what is being said. Of course, the resulting meaning will fit perfectly with the listener's own perspective as it is made up of components from their own map.

Being artfully vague and using metaphor and storytelling allows the speaker to use indirect suggestions that are more engaging for the listener and usually accepted into their map of the world more readily than direct commands. Now that you know this, you will probably want to find opportunities to use your new understanding, won't you?

# ACTIVITY PRACTISING YOUR PERSUASIVE LANGUAGE

Catch yourself just before you say the word *'but'* and substitute the word *'and'* instead. Notice the response you get from the other person.

Rather than saying something like '*I don't want to see the reception area looking so untidy and you so miserable again tomorrow*', why not say '*Tomorrow, when I walk into reception, I want to be impressed by the quiet calm and order that I see – as well as your big welcoming smile*'?

Have you ever told a story or anecdote about a similar situation to enlighten and transform thinking? What would it be like if you did? Imagine yourself doing just that and notice the difference that this will make for your team.

And before you finish reading this chapter, you can already hear yourself using these powerful language patterns effectively. Can't you?

# BODY LANGUAGE

> No mortal can keep a secret. If the lips are silent,
> he chatters with his fingertips; betrayal oozes
> out of every pore.
> SIGMUND FREUD

Have you ever watched someone's body language and wondered what that person was thinking or experiencing? Or caught yourself doing something like fiddling with your ring, pen or tapping your fingers? We communicate a lot via our body language.

POWERFUL USE OF LANGUAGE    121

## What is body language?

Body language is the process of communicating through conscious and unconscious gestures and movements. It is a way of transmitting information without words, through facial expressions, gestures, movements and posture. It is also linked to how we present ourselves: what we wear, our hairstyle, accessories and body art. In the main, people send and interpret body language signals unconsciously. We can get a strong sense of what another person is thinking or feeling from their body language.

The difference between verbal communication and non-verbal communication is that verbal communication is often well thought through and crafted to get the speaker's message across in line with their outcomes, whereas people are much less aware of their own non-verbal communication; therefore non-verbal communication can in some ways be considered a more honest or natural representation of what an individual is experiencing.

It is widely understood that human communication, especially communication linked to a person's emotional state, is usually conveyed most strongly via body language rather than through their words. Therefore, body language can give you a wealth of additional information compared with the words alone, provided you know how to read it.

## Why is body language important?

Non-verbal actions are powerful and they have meaning, which is why people still travel round the world for important business meetings to meet face to face. We have already seen that body language plays an important part in building effective rapport. By matching or mirroring the body language of the person you are talking to, you feel more connected. When this happens the conversation usually flows more easily too. As humans we do this naturally and unconsciously.

# Learning how to read body language

Can you tell the difference between someone who is relaxed and someone who is tense? Just think of the difference between someone enjoying a business lunch and someone who has just had their flight cancelled at the airport. You already know that *it is not possible to not communicate.*

It can be helpful to become aware of both your own and other people's body language. In particular, it can be helpful to make sure that your own body language is congruent with your spoken message. Saying that you are very pleased while frowning will send a confusing message to the person you are speaking to. Similarly, if you are listening to someone telling you that they are passionate about something and their body is very still, you may want to ask more questions because there appears to be a mismatch between body language and what is being said. Checking for congruence between the spoken message and the body-language message is a very helpful communication tool.

When you are talking to someone, you can consciously check the congruence of your overall message by ensuring that your words and body language are appropriately aligned. You can also check how your message has been received by your audience by observing their body language. Have they understood what you said to them? *The meaning of communication is the response you get* – and that is not just what you hear back from them; it is what you see too.

If you really want to get a sense of what is going on for another person you can get a lot of information by taking on their body posture. *Mind and body are part of the same system and anything that occurs in one part of the system will affect the other part.* Taking on another person's posture accurately can be very insightful. Next time you are in a meeting and you wonder how engaged a colleague is, discreetly take on their body language for a moment and you will get a sense of what is going on for them.

You can become much more consciously aware of body language by focusing your attention on people's posture, gestures and expressions. By using your sensory acuity to become more aware of body language, you can increase your understanding of what is going on for another person. Watching what people are doing, from big gestures to the tiny movements of their eyes and face, can help you establish a baseline so that you can calibrate and interpret the messages being transmitted by their body language. Different people will have different calibration; there are many different dialects of body language. Getting to know the body language and mannerisms of the people in your team can be a helpful way of establishing their baseline, so that, if they act out of character in body language terms, you will know that there is something going on for them and that gives you the option of asking questions to establish whether there is anything that they need or want to tell you.

## ACTIVITY DEVELOPING YOUR BODY LANGUAGE SKILLS

To develop your awareness of other people's body language you could start to pay attention to the body language around you in the office or your team and notice what is 'normal' for your colleagues.

You could pay conscious attention to the body language of the people you communicate with to get non-verbal feedback on how they are responding to you.

You could also pay more attention to your own body language and make minor changes and assess the impact of these different ways of communicating using body language.

Think about someone whom you want to understand more or have a better working relationship with. Accurately adopt their typical body posture. As you do this, notice where there is tension, where there is discomfort or what feels good. Having taken on their body posture, your own body has an experience of what it is like to hold that body posture and this is then transmitted to your mind. You now have access to more information and greater understanding of the individual. This is how actors are able to more easily take on the role of the character that they are playing.

# SUMMARY

- Building rapport with someone, being curious about their map of the world and asking them open questions about the structure of it (rather than focusing on the details of the content) is a great way to help them (and you) make sense of what they are thinking, feeling and doing.

- Asking open questions about someone's map of the world in this way acts as an 'undo' on the perceptual deletions, distortions and generalizations that they made when they constructed their map. When done with rapport this can be an enlightening and useful process that helps turn an impoverished map into a more useful, enriched map. This style of questioning is the basis of many forms of coaching.

- Using sensory-specific language, rich in visual, auditory and kinaesthetic words, is one way to help your communication become clearer and unambiguous to others; in a way which can be much more engaging and motivating than using highly abstract, generalized and 'educated' language.

- Be aware of the powerfully hypnotic effect of some words. Asking someone to 'try' to do something comes with an embedded message that you think they will fail. Also, the word 'but' acts as a powerful eraser on what was said previously. Consider whether 'and' would be a better conjunction. It provides more balance between what went before it and what comes after.

- Developing an awareness of your own and others' body language is the first step to being able to utilize this powerful communication channel which is usually left to the unconscious mind.

# BUSINESS APPLICATIONS

NLP tools and techniques can be very helpful and useful in the business world. This chapter provides practical examples of how you can use the NLP tools and techniques described in earlier chapters of this book to improve your effectiveness at work, whether you manage people, need to influence others or you would just like to be able to manage your boss better.

## FEEDBACK AND APPRAISALS

> The greatest good you can do for another is not to
> share your riches, but to reveal to him his own.
> BENJAMIN DISRAELI

Do you look forward to your appraisal or dread it? Do you seek out feedback or avoid it? Do you give feedback freely or withhold it? This chapter will explain the value of good feedback and give you the confidence to seek it out and give it *out in future.*

## What is feedback?

Feedback is information that we can use to learn how to do something better. In a business context feedback is important to encourage the behaviours and thinking that will help make the business a success. Generally, employees want feedback so that they know how well they are doing and what they need to do to improve their performance. Organizations use formal appraisal processes to give employees feedback, as well as regular meetings with their manager, together with feedback on a day-to-day basis. This ensures that employees know what is expected of them and how well they are doing. It also provides an opportunity for employees to give their manager and the organization feedback about their experience of working for that particular organization.

## What is so important about feedback?

All systems need feedback to adapt and survive. Without feedback it would be impossible to learn anything or improve what we currently do. By framing feedback as a gift rather than as criticism, we help ourselves and others to take on board the feedback and to use it to maximize our learning and improve our performance. It can be very tempting to argue with feedback or to feel hurt by it. To make the most of feedback, you need to frame it as helpful information which adds to the data that you already have about yourself. Being aware of and actively seeking feedback enables us to gain more accurate information about how we are proceeding towards our outcomes. Giving and receiving high-quality feedback in a work or personal situation will enable you to improve your performance and better achieve your outcomes. See Figure 6.1.

First, it can be helpful to hold the belief that *there is no failure, only feedback*. Failure is not usually a useful frame for moving forward and progressing. To help frame feedback as something that is useful rather than as criticism or failure, it can be helpful to ask a question to remind you both that the frame for the following

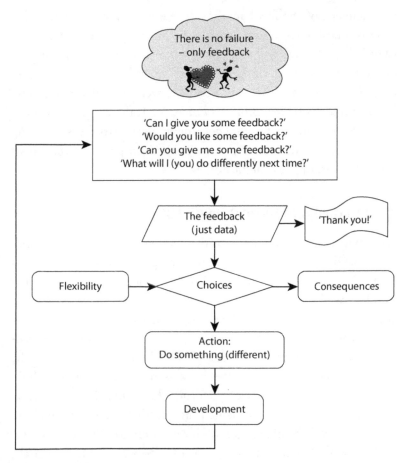

**Figure 6.1** Making the most of feedback

conversation is 'feedback' and set expectations accordingly. For example, 'I would welcome some feedback from you on how my presentation went' or 'Would you like some feedback on how I experienced your reaction to my proposal in that meeting?' Similarly, it is always a good idea to say 'Thank you' whenever you receive any feedback. After all, any data that you receive is useful information and you could always choose to ignore it. Sometimes the data that you receive as feedback will tell you more about the other person than it does about yourself. Assuming that the recipient of the feedback has developed some flexibility (it is usually helpful to assume that they have), then that feedback (which is just data) will give them some choices about what they do in the future. Each of those choices might have different consequences. In any case, the feedback has increased choice, and as you know, *choice is better than no choice*. What the recipient chooses to do next is up to them. They might decide to try something different and notice what that gives them in terms of their own development, or they might not.

## How to give and receive feedback

As a manager, you can give positive feedback whenever you think someone deserves it. Finding 'something good' to say to your staff every day can create a culture of praise as long as the 'something good' is well deserved and sincerely meant. Do not devalue your praise by giving it when it hasn't been earned.

As a manager, you also need to face up to giving negative feedback. Do it promptly and clearly. The longer you leave it, the harder it becomes. Giving feedback is much easier if you hold the belief that the feedback is helpful. Check that the information that you are about to give is helpful and that the person you are giving it to will be able to act on it and improve. You should also recognize that depriving someone of feedback denies them the opportunity to improve and develop. It might be helpful to note that studies have shown that there appears to be a 'magic ratio' of five appreciative comments to one critical comment that results in the greatest improvement in performance.

Some useful tips for giving feedback are:

- Ask yourself what your outcome is in giving the feedback. The only valid answer is in order to help and develop the other person. If you are doing it to score points or retaliate for some previous encounter, then your feedback is unlikely to be ecological and will probably not serve you or the recipient well.

- Asking the recipient if they would like some feedback, before you deliver it, will give them a chance to prepare themselves and put their own useful frame around what you are about to tell them.

- Give the feedback promptly.

- Do it in an appropriate environment.

- Maintain rapport.

- Give specific examples and be objective, referring to what you actually observed.

- Focus on the behaviour, not the person. When giving feedback about behaviour that you want to be different, it is helpful to remember that *a person's behaviour is not who they are.* Linking behaviour with their identity is unnecessary and unhelpful. There is a big difference between 'The child stole some sweets' and 'The child is a thief' or, taking an example from a business context, the difference between saying 'I think you lack commitment' and 'I have noticed that you leave early most days.'

- Acknowledge that your feedback is subjective in that it reflects the way that you experienced the recipient's behaviour.

- Give the recipient the opportunity to seek clarification.

- Aim for face to face and one to one.

- Feedback should always be honest.

- Use 'and' rather than 'but'.

- Make it first-hand. Own the feedback you give.

- It can be helpful to say what you would like to have happened instead. Give examples of what you would like to see, hear and feel so that the recipient is clear about your expectations. Doing this in sensory-specific language will help to avoid any ambiguity.

As an employee, being open to receiving feedback can be very conducive to helping you learn and adapt to meet the needs of the organization better. Remembering that the feedback is given with positive intentions to help you to improve can make it easier to accept the feedback.

Some useful tips for receiving feedback are:

- Frame it as useful information.

- Remember that feedback might tell you more about the person giving the feedback than it tells you about yourself.

- Maintain rapport with the giver and remember that giving feedback can be hard for some people. Saying 'Thank you' for the feedback will acknowledge that and help to encourage a feedback culture.

- You might want to ask some questions to help you understand how you could address the issues raised: 'How do you think this could be improved?', 'What do I need to change?', 'What would you prefer me to do?' It is less helpful to ask questions or make statements that challenge the feedback.

- If you find the feedback emotionally upsetting or painful, deal with the emotion first and then, when you feel better, go back to the feedback and decide whether you want to act on it or not.

Sometimes gifts are just what we want, sometimes they are practical and useful and sometimes they say more about the giver than the recipient. You can treasure the gift or put it aside to consider later or even throw it away. You have the same choices with feedback.

## THREE FEEDBACK MODELS

Here are three models for giving feedback which provide useful frameworks for effective conversational feedback.

## Start... stop... continue

Give specific examples of things you would like to see the recipient start doing/stop doing, and things that they already do that you would like them to continue. 'I would like to see you start arriving for meetings on time, to stop interrupting others so often and to continue to put in the preparation that you did for those agenda items.'

## More of... less of

Give specific example of things that the recipieint does that you would like to see more of and less of. 'I would like to see more examples of you listening to others and less of you talking at length about the issues that concern only you.'

## When you... I felt... I want... Will you...?

This model is very effective for feedback about behaviours that you would like to be different. 'When you shout at other people in the office, I feel upset and that you are being aggressive. I want you to keep your voice down and talk in a normal tone and volume. Will you do that?'

Furthermore, you can add 'If you do that, then...' and 'If you don't do that, then...' to this model. This can help to add clarity about the consequences for the individual of making the requested change, or not. This can be useful in cases where more formal disciplinary action or a performance procedure is being followed. Organizational cultures which encourage and expect regular feedback tend to score highly on employee engagement measures and this has a positive impact on performance and productivity.

# ACTIVITY  IMPROVING YOUR FEEDBACK SKILLS

- Practise giving appreciative feedback to someone that you have not given feedback to before. Catch them out doing something good.

- It can be helpful to understand your own reaction to feedback. What is your own response when you are given feedback? Are you defensive? Do you tend to dismiss feedback or argue with it? What difference does it make who you get the feedback from? Are you open to feedback? What can you do differently to encourage people to give you feedback, which will help you to learn and improve? What beliefs would be helpful in supporting you to develop the flexibility to receive feedback and act on it?

- You could ask a colleague to enter into a mutual feedback process with you around specific aspects at work. Within this arrangement you could ask them to give you some feedback on your feedback to them. What else could you do to get some feedback on your feedback-giving skills?

- Does your company have a formal feedback and appraisal system? How could it be improved? What are you going to do differently now?

## SUMMARY

- Feedback is information that we can choose to use to adjust what we are doing to get a different (usually better) outcome. Without feedback we would find it very difficult to learn, improve and communicate. Think of it as a gift!

- Always say 'thank you' when you receive feedback. It is useful information about either you or the person who gave it to you, and you always have choice about whether to act on it. It might have been difficult for the person to give you that feedback. If you want more feedback in future from this person, make sure they know that you appreciate it.

- Feedback is more effective when given in rapport.

- Think about how you deliver feedback so that it is most effective to the recipient. There are some useful linguistic models for giving feedback.

# THE VISION THING: 'I HAVE A DREAM'

To grasp and hold a vision, that is the very essence of successful leadership – not only on the movie set where I learned it, but everywhere.
RONALD REAGAN

We can all think of people who have captured our imagination and inspired us to try something new or to persevere with an ambition or project. At times we will need to do this at work and it can be helpful to understand what constitutes a vision and how you convey this so that it inspires and enthuses your audience.

## What is a vision?

A vision is an idea that is perceived vividly in the imagination. One of the most famous visions was expressed by Dr Martin Luther King Jr in his 1963 Lincoln Memorial speech, 'I have a dream', when he called for racial harmony and an end to discrimination in America. In this speech Martin Luther King described specifically what he would see, hear and feel 'one day' when his outcome was achieved. Many business leaders have a vision which drives their business ambition and shapes the organization. Having a shared vision is one of the ways that they engage their people and motivate them to achieve this.

## When is having a vision important?

You can have a vision for yourself, for your team, for your organization or for society. If you need others to contribute to the achievement of your vision, you need to be able to communicate it in such a way that it becomes a shared vision and engages people to the extent that they are moved to action. This is the challenge of many managers and business leaders.

## Communicating your vision

Setting out your vision is how you lead people towards a clear and compelling outcome. Effective leaders are able to communicate by using persuasive and sensory-specific language to convey their message to their audience in a way that engages them so that they share the vision. The leader makes the vision real for people by providing evidence of what it will be like when the vision is achieved: what they will see, hear and feel.

Being careful to tailor your message to your audience will help you get your message across. Using a range of sensory-specific language throughout the communication of your vision will help you engage your audience. Remember that a significant number of your audience will have a visual preference and these people will need pictures and diagrams to make sense of your vision. You will need to paint the picture for them. Another section of your audience will have a kinaesthetic preference and will need to feel connected to and part of the vision. It will be important to them that the vision sets out how people will feel when the vision is achieved. Finally, some of your audience will have an auditory preference and will want your message to ring true for them and for the vision to be in harmony with their own values. For these people your vision will need to sound right too.

To communicate your vision effectively you will also want to address different patterns of thinking. People who have an away-from preference will want to know that you have considered the risks and the potential hazards involved in achieving the vision. Those who prefer to mismatch will want to know what other options were considered and why this vision was chosen. People with a detail preference will need you to break down your vision into manageable steps, probably starting with where you are currently, briefly outlining the vision and then returning to the steps and milestones necessary to achieve the vision.

People with a preference for similarity will need to know what will stay the same as their current experience when the vision is achieved. What will they be able to hold on to for stability as any changes are introduced? People with a preference for difference will be motivated by what is new and different compared with the current arrangements.

The more you can connect with people's beliefs and values and their identity, the more likely they are to buy into your vision and to be able to see, hear and feel themselves playing their own part in the achievement of the vision.

By setting out a clear and compelling vision, you are providing people with a sense of direction. This will enable them to make empowered decisions based on the best way to achieve the vision in their current circumstances. They are likely to need to use their flexibility to achieve the vision, rather like a sailor who sets sail for a destination and has to negotiate tides, currents, changes in wind direction and strength and other boats on the water. While the most direct route between A and B may be to take a straight-line course, this may not be possible particularly if it requires sailing straight into the wind. Instead, a competent sailor will keep their focus on the destination and work to optimize their course, to make the most of the prevailing conditions, continually adjusting the sails and the course in response to feedback, always with B as the desired destination.

## ACTIVITY DEVELOPING YOUR OWN VISIONARY STYLE

- What kind of visionary or inspirational person or leader do you want to be?

- How do you see yourself developing your own visionary style? What will you see, hear and feel yourself doing when you are inspiring others?

- How will you ensure that your outcome is both well formed and compelling, both for yourself and others? What tools, techniques and methodologies will you be using?

- What language will you use to capture the imagination and commitment of all the people that are important or significant in making your outcome happen?

- How will you make the most of your imagination to do that? What will you need to do specifically to become the visionary and inspirational person you want to be?

- What will be the biggest challenges for you and where will you need to further develop your flexibility?

## SUMMARY

- Being able to develop and articulate a clear vision or outcome is an effective way to motivate and inspire yourself and others.

- Use sensory-specific language and think about how you might need to tailor your vision so that it sits comfortably in others' maps of the world.

# SELLING

If you are not moving closer to what you want in sales
(or in life), you probably aren't doing enough asking.
JACK CANFIELD

We are all sold to on a daily basis and most of us need to be able to persuade and influence others in order to be successful in our roles. NLP techniques have been used in effective selling for years and many of the tools that we have set out earlier in this book are used to sell effectively.

## What is selling?

Selling is about persuading and influencing others to buy your products, services, arguments or ideas.

## Why is being able to sell useful?

Being able to sell is not just about exchanging your products or services for money. Selling includes being able to influence and persuade others to appreciate and understand your ideas and thinking. If you can sell your ideas and influence others, you can achieve your outcomes and those of your organization.

## How to improve your selling

Many inexperienced salespeople will spend their time telling people about their product, service or idea. Yet the most successful sales-people ask far more questions when they engage with prospective customers than simply spending time telling people about what they have for sale.

Most people are interested in things that are important in their own world and their problems and circumstances. These people often respond well to someone else taking an interest in their map of the world. By asking people what they think or feel about something, you can gather information that helps you identify what it is that your product, service or idea can do specifically for this person – especially if you do this with rapport. Let the customer do the talking. What is the problem or issue that your product or service solves or makes better? Finding out as much as you can about the other person, helps you to tailor your message to meet their needs in a way that they are most receptive to hearing.

They will know exactly what they mean when they use certain words from their own map of the world. If you use their words they will think and feel that you know exactly what they mean too. When you notice their sensory language (see, hear, feel) and match their preferences in your responses, you are more likely to connect with them and this will help you build great rapport. Also, if you identify their patterns of thinking preferences you can tailor your message to reflect these. It is easy to sell life insurance to someone who has an away-from thinking pattern, who does not want their family to be left in financial difficulty if they should die. You can also major on the similarities or difference between your product and a competitor's product depending on whether you have identified the person as having a difference- or similarity-thinking pattern preference.

The first step to effective selling is to do your preparation. In preparing for a sales meeting, be very clear about your outcome. Before the meeting do your research so that you know what the issues are likely to be. Keep an open mind so that if your research is wrong or out of date, you can listen to the customer and understand their issues. Find out what the customer's problems are and what they would like to have happen. What is most important to them? Actively listen to their answer because they will tell you – you just need to hear them. Remember the words, phrases and metaphors that they use. This is the language that makes sense to them and they will be most receptive to. Be prepared to use their language when you explain how your product or service will meet their needs.

Next, really understand what frustrates your customer and what keeps them awake at night or would make their life easier or better.

What is it that they want? What is their desired outcome? You might need to ask them if they are the sort of person who prefers to talk mostly about what they don't want. Finally, once you understand your customer's map of the world and their issues, you can adapt how and what you tell them about your product or service or ideas to meet their needs. With the information you gathered in discussion you can be very clear about how you can help your customer.

The customer cares about their problems, not yours, and they are interested in the solutions to their problems. Asking the right open questions means that you steer and control the conversation and the customer's thinking. For example, you could say, 'You mentioned you were having problems with X and that you wanted Y, how will you know that you have found the best solution to your problem?' This question encourages the customer to tell you their buying criteria. Once you have this you can use it as a checklist in explaining the features and benefits of your product. By asking open questions you direct their attention to the issues and problems that your product, service or ideas can solve. Now it would be helpful to hold the belief that *there is a solution to every problem.*

By building rapport, demonstrating a genuine interest in the customer and sharing the problems they face, you are in a position to work with them to develop a solution. Working together on a solution is a lot better than working against each other.

## ACTIVITY  PUTTING IT INTO PRACTICE

- If you could do one thing to improve your current selling technique, what would that be?
- The next time you want to sell something to someone, what will you do differently? And what else?

# SUMMARY

- In NLP terms we think of selling as 'facilitated buying'.

- How can we most effectively meet the needs of the customer?

- What problem are they trying to solve?

- What does their map of the world need?

- What is their desired outcome? Then, and only then, we can start to describe how our product or service might meet their need and desired outcome.

# CHOOSING THE MOST EFFECTIVE LEADERSHIP STYLE FOR THE SITUATION

There are times when we are required to show leadership and it can be helpful to have an understanding of our own preferred style and also the extent of our flexibility in utilizing different styles in different situations.

## What is leadership?

Leadership is the ability to inspire others to deliver outcomes. There are many different leadership styles and techniques and some are more effective than others, depending on the situation. You can be a leader whether you are leading one person or thousands of people.

## What sort of leader do you want to be?

Many of the techniques described in this book are used by effective leaders. For example, leaders need to be able to set out a clear vision of where they are taking their team or organization. To do this they need to use towards thinking to develop a clear and compelling outcome. Knowing where they are going and what it will be like when they get there helps them to persuade others to invest their efforts in achieving the leader's and the organization's outcome. Leaders need to be able to communicate the vision and to influence and engage their team or workforce to work towards achieving the organization's outcomes. They also need to be able to build great rapport with the people that they are leading.

Leaders need the flexibility to use both persuasive language to convince people of the possibility and benefits of their vision and specific language to clarify understanding. Great leaders often have good self-awareness and the ability to manage themselves as well as the skills to manage others highly effectively. Being able to stand in the shoes of your people and appreciate their maps of the world is another useful skill adopted by successful leaders.

So how can you do all of that? How can you be flexible and adapt to others' maps of the world and yet maintain your integrity, authenticity and authority? How do you know which technique or tool to adopt in any given situation? How do you decide which approach to take when the pressure is on? What style of leadership will work best for you now?

## A wide range of leadership styles

It can be useful to think of leadership styles along a continuum from directive to non-directive approaches. See Figure 6.2.

**Figure 6.2**  The leadership continuum

It is useful to appreciate the range of leadership interventions and styles that could be adopted so that you can identify the style that best suits each particular situation. Of course, it is also useful to recognize that the different leadership styles require the leader be flexible in their approach. It would be helpful to gain an appreciation of where your current comfort zones and boundaries are with respect to the different styles. You will undoubtedly have a preferred style and there will be other styles that are more of a stretch for you. Having the flexibility to deploy a particular style in a particular situation will increase your range and potentially your effectiveness as a leader.

As you move along the leadership continuum from directive to non-directive styles, the relationship between the leader and the person being led changes. It can be useful to consider how the following elements change at each point along the continuum:

- How the relationship between leader and led is set up.

- What is the nature of the leadership relationship itself? Who is the expert? Who has the authority? How much trust is necessary for this style to work?

- What is the contract between the leader and the follower? What structure, rules and understandings need to be in place to support this style of leadership?

- What are the conversations and language used? What is the proportion of time spent giving answers compared to the time spent asking questions? Who is asking questions and who is giving answers?

- Who owns the outcomes? Who is responsible when things go wrong? How motivated does the follower need to be?

- What are the beliefs held by each party that support this style? What are the beliefs about each other? What are the beliefs about the organization? What are the beliefs about the outcomes?

# Choosing the most appropriate style

Think of a specific leadership situation and consider which point on the leadership continuum is the most effective or appropriate place to be to achieve your outcome. Here are some example situations:

- setting an individual's objectives;

- solving a technical problem;

- explaining the expenses-claim procedures to a new employee;

- introducing a change programme;

- selling your vision of where the organization needs to be in five years' time;

- making people aware of an important health and safety issue;

- helping someone in your team explore potential solutions to an issue that they have;

- delegating a task where the outcome is clear and there is a choice about how to deliver the outcome.

To successfully deploy your chosen style of leadership it is helpful to signpost which approach you are taking to the person you are leading. Being clear about which style you intend to adopt is really important. Often leadership issues and misunderstandings arise when the leader and the follower assume that they are on different points along the continuum. If you are using a more directive approach, then you need to frame this clearly with the other person so that they are clear about your expectations of them. Similarly, if you are expecting others to feel empowered to make their own decisions about how they deliver the outcomes, this needs to be flagged and understood by both sides. In order to take full advantage of the range of styles at your disposal, you will need to ensure that both sides are working at the same position. This will need to be communicated and agreed between both sides for that style to be most effective.

Stephen was a great employee, conscientious and willing, he would get his work done quickly and was always asking for more work. David, his manager, liked Stephen and wanted him to develop in his role. David felt that Stephen needed to think for himself a bit more and stop asking David, 'What else needs to be done?'

David sat down with Stephen at a one-to-one meeting and gave him feedback that he was doing a great job. David explained that Stephen now needed to move from wanting to be told what to do, to working out what needed to be done for himself. David agreed to coach Stephen to help him achieve this.

The next time Stephen asked David, 'What do you want me to do now?' David replied, 'What do you think needs doing?' Stephen had to stop and think for a moment and then he came up with several suggestions. David explored each suggestion with Stephen, who then went off and did the tasks he had identified. David repeated this process for a few days and soon Stephen was confident to work out for himself what needed to be done.

## ACTIVITY FINDING AND ADOPTING THE OPTIMUM LEADERSHIP STYLE

- What is your favourite or most effective leadership style along this continuum as a leader? How do you prefer to be led?

- If the style you normally use is not currently working for you (you are not getting your outcome), then think about using your flexibility to move along the continuum. What else needs to change for you to move from your preferred position and be a more effective leader?

- What flexibility does the person you are communicating with or managing have to move along the continuum? What are your limits? The other person's limits? Does your organization or culture prevent you from adopting certain leadership styles? What can you do to increase the range of styles that are available to you?

## SUMMARY

- There is a wide spectrum of ways in which we can relate to people in a management or leadership situation.

- It can be helpful to think about what style is most appropriate for the given situation. Be aware of your preferences and the 'norms' or preferences of the organization that you are in, and the people that you are leading.

- Then, you will need to 'contract' with the follower(s) to make sure that they are happy to be the recipient of the style that you want to adopt.

- As you lead in that style, be aware of the feedback, including results that you get and re-contract and adjust appropriately.

# MODELLING OTHERS' ABILITIES

And as we let our own light shine, we unconsciously give other people permission to do the same.
NELSON MANDELA

Have you ever been curious about how another person can do something really well; a particular skill or approach that they take that works very well for them? Have you ever wished that you could do what they can do? It is possible to identify how someone does something and to adopt their approach to be able to do what they do.

## What is modelling?

NLP has its origins in modelling how some very effective communicators did what they did. Modelling is the process of identifying and describing, in a useful way, those patterns that make up a useful ability. Once those patterns have been identified and described, then others can acquire the ability simply by following the 'instructions' in the model. You already know that *if one person can do something, then anyone can learn how to do it.*

## Why you might want to model an ability

Have you ever admired the way that someone has done something and then asked them how they did it? You might have got the answer 'I don't know... I just did it', because abilities are often performed unconsciously, particularly when people have practised them and become very good at doing them. Modelling provides a methodology for helping you to 'unpick' a useful ability, in yourself or others, in a way that would be helpful for other people to acquire.

We often believe that some people are born with certain talents. They are able to 'naturally' perform certain tasks in an effortless way. Similarly, other people may develop a proficiency in an ability without being born with such a talent. They learnt to do so from their life experiences and have taught themselves patterns of perceiving, thinking and behaving required to perform that ability. Modelling provides a framework for describing those patterns that are required to manifest such an ability. It is the process of analysing what a person does and believes in order to perform that ability.

## How to model an ability

Any ability can be broken down into a number of elements as shown in Figure 6.3. These elements link together and contribute to being able to perform that ability. Most 'How to' text books

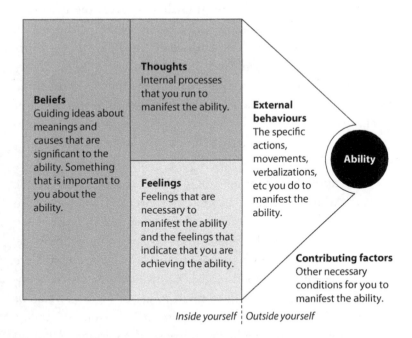

**Figure 6.3**   Modelling an ability
Source: Gordon and Graham (2005).

and manuals focus mainly on those external behaviours that are directly observable outside the body. Although these specific actions, movements and language patterns often play an important role in performing the ability, they often miss the thoughts, feelings and beliefs that also make a significant, if not pivotal, contribution to being able to manifest the ability really well. Sometimes these thoughts, feelings and beliefs occur at an unconscious level.

NLP provides a useful framework for finding out or eliciting those 'invisible' elements that often turn out to be 'the difference that makes the difference' in being able to perform the ability effectively.

## Using the meta-model to unpick an ability

The meta-model is a methodology of questioning that asks open questions from an 'outside' position that recovers the deletions, distortions and generalizations in someone's map of the world. It can also help you to be very specific about the patterns of perceiving, thinking and behaving required to perform an ability effectively. Asking open questions that start with the words 'How' and 'What' about the ability is a great way to build the model of the ability.

### Beliefs

The motivation that drives any ability will come from a core value or belief. Asking the question 'What's important to you when you are (performing the ability)?' will usually elicit that value or belief.

Any ability is usually linked back to some higher purpose. Knowing what that higher purpose is and how it is evaluated are essential elements of a good model. You can ask 'And what's important about that?' up to three times to get to the core value or belief that drives the motivation behind a behaviour or ability. Once you have found the higher purpose, then asking 'What do you see, hear or feel that lets you know that there is (the higher purpose)?' would be a helpful question to ask at this point.

For example, someone who is very good at public speaking might say that what is important to them about being able to do that is 'making a personal connection with each member of the audience' and that the evidence for making that connection is 'seeing smiling faces, people nodding as I speak, hearing only my own voice and feeling that sense of connection'. That is the evidence that the role model uses to confirm that they have reached their outcome. Of course, you can continue to ask open questions to be even more specific about what the person feels that tells them there is that connection or how they know there is sufficient connection to make them feel that it has been an effective communication.

## Thoughts

These are usually called 'strategies' in NLP and are the sequences of steps and tests that we think about when doing something. Some good questions to elicit this part of the model are: 'How do you go about (performing the ability)?', 'What do you do when that isn't working?', 'How do you know when to start/stop that?'

You can make up your own questions appropriate to the ability you are modelling as long as you follow the basic rule that good model-elicitation questions refer to the process of the ability rather than the content of what they are actually doing and that the best questions usually start with 'How', 'What', 'Where' or 'When'. Your aim in asking these questions is to establish the strategy that the person uses to perform the ability.

## Feelings

Often a certain feeling, state or sequence of states will be required to perform the ability well. Here are some good example questions for eliciting this part of the model: 'What is the background feeling that keeps you engaged in (performing the ability)?', 'What feelings do you notice that tell you that you need to change what you are doing to keep (performing the ability)?'

Answers to these questions will give you an insight into what feelings and sequence of feelings need to be present to keep on performing the ability well.

### External behaviour

This element is usually the main focus of questioning when trying to learn how to do something new: 'What are you doing that is essential to (performing the ability)?' The answer will tell you what you need to do to perform the behaviour.

### Contributing factors

It can be helpful to check that you have asked all the necessary questions. The person who has the ability will usually tell you if you have missed anything significant when you ask: 'And is there anything else I didn't ask you about (performing the ability) that I ought to have?'

## Acquiring the model yourself

Once you have elicited the elements that make up someone else's model for performing an ability, you can acquire and implement the model yourself. You can try on each element of the model individually at first to check how well it fits and what you need to flex and adapt in order to hold or perform that element. As you add all of the elements together you may notice that you have to stretch and flex in certain areas to maintain the model.

Acquiring someone else's model will usually require you to develop some flexibility in your own patterns and preferences. As you know, you have your own set of preferred patterns of thinking, feeling and behaving, not to mention your own beliefs about what is true, all of which are unique to you. You might need to adopt and refine some of your non-preferred patterns in order to perform an ability more effectively. For example, an enthusiasm for detail and a focus on others' needs rather than your own might be helpful patterns to adopt when manifesting the ability to 'listen with empathy'. A good model, together with some knowledge about your own preferences, will help you to highlight those areas where you need to develop your own flexibility in order to perform well at the ability. For example, holding the belief that 'I am the sort of person who can (perform the ability)' might just be the difference that makes the difference and gives you the necessary confidence to do that very thing.

## ACTIVITY  WHERE ARE YOU GOING TO START?

- What ability would you like to acquire? Who do you know that is a born 'natural' at doing that? Or who do you know that has learnt how to do that really well?

- Perhaps it is an ability to sell or cold call, to present confidently to a large audience, to delegate tasks effectively to team members, to find the motivation to study while doing a full-time job, to come to a decision or to switch off at the weekend and not think about work at all.

- Which ability would you choose to model first?

## SUMMARY

- NLP is based on modelling some of the useful communication abilities of others and adopting or acquiring those strategies, states and behaviours yourself.

- Often an ability is critically dependent on what is going on 'on the inside' rather than simply the behaviours that you can see going on 'on the outside'.

- People who are very good at an ability often are unconscious of what is going on 'on the inside'.

- Open questions and curiosity are a good way of 'unpicking' an exemplar's model of how they manifest an ability.

- To adopt someone else's model to perform an ability, you will probably need to adjust your own preferences and habits as you learn to notice, think, feel, assume and behave in new ways.

# STRESS MANAGEMENT: BUILDING PERSONAL RESILIENCE

An obvious fact about negative feelings is often overlooked. They are caused by us, not by external happenings. An outside event presents the challenge but we react to it. So we must attend to the way we take things – not to the things themselves.
VERNON HOWARD

We have probably all experienced stressful times or events at work. Have you noticed that some people seem to be able to bounce back quickly from an exceptionally demanding period at work whilst others take longer and are more adversely affected by the experience? It can be helpful to understand our own responses to stress and it can be useful to develop some techniques for building our personal resilience so that we can deal with stressful situations appropriately.

## What is personal resilience?

Personal resilience is the ability to bounce back from setbacks, to be able to find the opportunity in every challenge and to think positively about what you can learn from a negative experience. Our level of personal resilience will affect the level of stress that we are able to deal with without it having an adverse effect on our lives and those of the people around us.

## Why is personal resilience useful?

In an ever-changing and unpredictable world, stuff happens, and we have to be able to deal with it. Our ability to deal with it well and to be able to get on with our lives and work, rather than be adversely affected by events, depends on our levels of resilience. Those with a more positive or robust attitude are more able to deal with life's setbacks. Despite experiencing major trauma, people with high levels of resilience are able to integrate this experience and get on with the rest of their lives. This is not about being unemotional or denying this experience; rather it is about facing difficulties and dealing with them.

Our reaction to stress is linked to the basic human instinct to survive. Human beings are programmed to detect danger and to respond to ensure their survival. This is called the 'freeze, flight or fight' reflex. In primitive times, when we detected a threat, our reaction would be to immediately freeze: notice how someone jumps and then freezes at the sound of a loud unexpected bang. The freeze reflex occurs in response to a perceived threat, and adrenaline and cortisol flood the body so that it is ready to flee or fight as required.

In many cases, staying still was enough to deter a predator programmed to detect movement. If freezing did not ensure safety, then the next choice was flight: to run away. If this option was not viable, the final option was to stay and fight for survival. While this was no doubt helpful in earlier times, the same responses can cause difficulties in today's working environment, particularly if we continually flood our bodies with adrenaline and cortisol and then don't need it to flee or physically fight.

Stress is defined as the body's reaction to a stressor, real or imagined. Often we are able to cope with a certain amount of stress and some people need a certain degree of stress to move into action. However, if the stress increases and/or is present for a prolonged period of time, we can become distressed and start to feel an adverse impact both physically and psychologically.

## How to build personal resilience

It is helpful to be able to manage our response to stress. We can do that by developing our personal resilience, paying attention to our well-being and ensuring that our approach to life and our strategies for achieving in life are helpful and useful to us.

The most significant factor affecting stress is a feeling of lack of control. As soon as you feel overwhelmed and out of control, stress levels increase. Remaining calm and feeling in control are the most effective ways of dealing with stress. This requires an element of state management and clarity about your outcome and your plans to achieve your outcome. You can develop strategies for handling stress and ensure that the choices you make when you feel stressed are healthy choices rather than short-term fixes such as drinking or eating too much.

Stress management is also about your attitude to stress. If you think stress is a necessary part of getting things done, then you may see it as a positive thing as long as it stays at reasonable levels. Alternatively, if you constantly describe yourself as stressed and believe that that is part of who you are, then this will have a more debilitating effect on you. There is a big difference between describing yourself as exhibiting stress-related behaviours and defining yourself as stressed. Remember the presupposition *a person's behaviour is not who they are.*

Being able to reframe situations and your own levels of stress to a more positive frame can be helpful and enable you to cope more effectively with high workloads or difficult situations: for example, '*I feel overloaded with work but at least I have work to do rather than being out of work like so many people affected by the economic downturn.*'

Being able to focus on your desired outcome will enable you to cope with significant stress, if the achievement of that outcome is compelling. Think of people who hold down a full-time job, have a family and find time to study for further qualifications that will help them advance their careers or people that work 15 hours a day to develop their own business.

The key to developing personal resilience is to develop your self-awareness to know what stresses you and how you react to stressful situations and then to work to develop new strategies and resourceful states that will assist you in dealing with these situations more effectively in the future. If working to a tight deadline energizes you, that is a great strategy for you. If it causes you significant stress, then it is important to plan ahead and prioritize so that you can deliver the work ahead of the deadline. It is also helpful to plan recovery time to allow you to recharge after a particularly busy period or stressful time.

People who have high levels of resilience are generally more optimistic about life without losing touch with reality. They look for the opportunities in difficulties rather than the difficulties in opportunities. In looking for the positives in every situation they will ask themselves, 'How can I learn from this?' or 'How can I think about this differently and in a more helpful way?' Both are good examples of helpful reframes.

## ACTIVITY  PUTTING IT INTO PRACTICE

- Review which situations you find stressful. What is the stimulus or trigger which causes you to feel stressed and what is your usual response to that trigger? How could you help yourself choose a different attitude to that trigger in the future?

- What if you could consider how you react to periods of stress and whether your reactions add to or reduce your stress levels? Do you work late to catch up and cut back on the time you usually spend exercising and then sleep badly or do you take time out to reprioritize work, cut down on alcohol, make time for exercise and get plenty of sleep? Paying attention to your needs and looking after yourself will improve your resilience and your capacity to deal with stress.

- Who do you know who handles stress well, who you could model in order to develop your own levels of resilience?

## SUMMARY

- Outcome thinking and adopting some behavioural flexibility are good ways to deal with stress.

- Becoming more aware of your own physiology and state (how you feel) are also useful ways of helping you decide when you need to start doing things differently.

## TIME MANAGEMENT

Being outcome focused about how you spend your time and how you utilize your energy can make a significant difference to your efficiency and effectiveness and help you achieve your outcomes.

# What is time management?

Time is a constant and there is no way of increasing or decreasing time. However, what you do with your time and what energy you choose to invest as you use your time is up to you. Time management is about making best use of your time and achieving more in the time available. It is about gaining more control over your time and making sure that you concentrate on what is important to you and that you don't waste time on the irrelevant. To do this well you need to have a clear outcome and focus your energy on achieving that outcome.

# Why is time management useful?

Consciously managing the way you both spend your time and utilize your energy can increase both your efficiency and effectiveness. Time management is a combination of planning, prioritizing, delegating and controlling your environment as well as understanding your patterns, routines and beliefs about time, and utilizing these to achieve your outcomes.

Time management is an important skill that contributes to improved work satisfaction and lower stress levels as well as improved quality of work and increased productivity. People who manage their time well tend to make fewer mistakes and proactively manage their work rather than resorting to crisis management continually. Effective time management can improve the quality of your whole life and the lives of the people around you.

# How to manage your time

One of the keys to successful time management is to be clear about your outcome, so that you can direct your energy and time to focus on that outcome. Ensuring that your outcome is well formed and compelling, so that you are motivated to achieve it, is helpful. Once you know what you want, you need to plan your time to

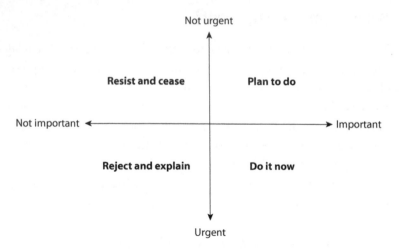

**Figure 6.4**   Time management

achieve your outcome. Having a plan and sticking to it will increase the chances of your achieving your outcome and will require you to protect your time and energy and to make conscious decisions about how you use both your time and your energy.

Being able to judge whether something is urgent or important is crucial for good time management. See Figure 6.4. You need to aim to spend most of your time on important things, and ideally the majority of your energy and focus needs to be on the important and not yet urgent. Noticing how you use your time and energy and what steals your time and energy is a great way of identifying how to use your time and energy more effectively.

Take a moment to consider how you have spent your time over the last day or week. When were you most productive? How much of your time was spent on activities from each of the different levels of importance and urgency categories? What was your focus on? What did you believe about the time available to you? How were your energy levels? When did they feel high and when did they feel low?

Reviewing how you spend your time and energy can raise your consciousness of when you are most effective and how you are when you are most productive. People who have high focus and energy tend to be quite purposeful about the action and choices they make regarding how they spend their time. Because they have high focus they are able to differentiate between activity that adds value and activity that wastes time. These people can be described as 'purposeful action takers' and they are usually calm and reflective and consistent even in a crisis. These people believe in planning ahead and being very clear about their outcomes and what they expect from others. Purposeful action takers are often in short supply in organizations that tend to have many more high-energy and low-focus people. These high-energy and low-focus people can be described as 'busy managers' and they are often quite distracted and frenetic. They will tell you how busy they are and how there is never enough time in the day. These 'busy managers' can be seen as role models and 'infect' the people that they manage so that they too become frenzied and distracted. These people can be developed to have higher focus by being encouraged to be clearer about their outcomes and to regularly review how they focus their energy and use their time. By doing this they can move to become purposeful action takers.

We have already seen in the section on patterns of thinking that some people have a preference for planning ahead and working to a clear schedule (the people with a judging preference in Myers-Briggs terms) and others have a preference for keeping their options open and being energized by the last-minute rush to get their work done (the people with a perceiving preference in Myers-Briggs terms). The people with a judging preference prefer to plan ahead and like to build in contingency time for emergencies. They generally believe that having a plan is the key to delivering a project on time and that without a plan everything just drifts before a last-minute panic, which is stressful and unhelpful. In contrast, the people with a perceiving preference tend to believe that they are at their most creative when they are up against a deadline and that a plan is constraining and rigid. Knowing your own preferred patterns can help you identify what you may need to do differently in future to achieve your outcomes more successfully, if your current approach is not helping you. Once you understand your own preferences you can explore with your colleagues their preferences and what they need from you in order to deliver a joint project on time.

## ACTIVITY BECOMING A PURPOSEFUL ACTION TAKER

- What do you need to do to become more of a purposeful action taker?

- What if you reviewed your outcomes to ensure that they were well formed and compelling?

- What if you became more aware of your energy levels and the most effective time of day for tackling certain activities and you planned your day around these times where possible?

- Part of protecting your time for proactive work is learning to say 'no' with rapport and explaining constructively that you have no capacity to do what has been requested or that you cannot meet the deadline or that you are not the right person for this task or that you don't think the task needs to be done. How well do you do this now and how can you improve your ability to say 'no'?

- Focus and energy are resourceful states for good time management. How could you acquire those states when you need to?

# SUMMARY

- Standing back, in third position, and making conscious decisions about how you spend your time, rather than just being in it, can be a helpful process.

- Whilst stood back, become aware of the importance and the urgency of all the tasks that face you and decide which to do next.

- Becoming more aware of your own states and thinking preferences can help you manage your energy levels to better match the demands of your work. Match those demanding tasks to the times when you have the energy appropriate for that task.

- An understanding of other peoples' preferences and patterns regarding time management will help you better plan and work with them.

# FURTHER NLP RESOURCES AND TRAINING OPPORTUNITIES

You might have found this book helpful and now want to take your learning about NLP a little bit further. You might be asking yourself: How else could NLP help me?, What else can I read?, What courses might it be useful to attend? This chapter is intended to help you find some answers to those questions.

## BOOKS ABOUT NLP

There are lots of books and materials available on the internet about NLP, from 'self help' to story books right through to those with a more 'academic' or textbook style. It is difficult to recommend from such a vast list without knowing the readers' specific objectives. That said, some of the classic NLP texts can help to provide an invaluable foundation in the philosophy, skills and principles of NLP.

The very early books by Richard Bandler and John Grinder, such as *Reframing* (Bandler and Grinder, 1982), *Using your Brain for a Change* (Bandler, 1985), *Trance-formations* (Grinder and Bandler, 1981) and *Frogs into Princes* (Bandler and Grinder, 1979), all give a useful insight into the roots and development of NLP. And for the brave, *The Structure of Magic*, Vols 1 and 2 (Bandler and Grinder, 1975/76) gives an exhaustive breakdown of the development of what became the NLP meta-model.

Robert Dilts is also a much published author of NLP books. Two of his earlier works which have become 'classic' NLP texts are *Changing Belief Systems with NLP* (1990) and *Sleight of Mouth* (1999).

Some of the books by Michael Hall and Bob G Bodenhamer are useful manual style books including *The Sourcebook of Magic* (Hall, 2004) and *The User's Manual for the Brain*, Vols 1 and 2 (Bodenhamer and Hall, 2001).

A good next step after this book would be Joseph O'Connor and John Seymour's *Introducing NLP* (1990) which is a good Practitioner level text.

# NLP TRAINING AND CERTIFICATION STANDARDS

There is no single organization that manages the formal accreditation of NLP training or certification. Hence, there is no official course content, duration or defined levels of competency, ethical standards or principles. However, there are a number of organizations that have set their own standards that reflect how they believe NLP should be taught, practised and accredited. Similarly, there are other bodies and organizations that run NLP courses that do not affiliate themselves with any of these standards or bodies. Some of the larger accreditation organizations are:

*The Association of NLP (ANLP)* – A UK based organization which recognizes NLP certified trainers that also complete their recognized trainers scheme.

*The American Board of NLP (ABNLP)* – A US based organization which is an adjunct to the American Board of Hypnotherapy.

*The International NLP Training Association (INLPTA)* – An international cooperative organization which defines a set of standards of quality, professionalism and ethics in its NLP training and conduct of business.

*The Professional Guild of NLP* – A UK and Australian organization whose members agree to adhere to a common training approach, code of ethics and principles.

# NLP TRAINING COURSES

There are lots of NLP training courses available. From those offering 'covert seduction techniques', right through to fully accredited and certified courses for coaching, training, therapy or business applications. The more formal and traditional NLP training courses fall into four levels of accredited and certified training.

*Diploma* – Usually a five-day course covering many of the basic NLP models and techniques. This book covers much of what might be included on a NLP Diploma course. Such a course will give you an opportunity to practise the techniques with others and receive feedback from experienced NLP trainers.

*Practitioner* – These courses typically run over several months and include a minimum of 15 days formal classroom training. Certification to NLP Practitioner level is usually based on the process of feedback, learning and integration of attitudes, skills and knowledge rather than examination. However, some courses will include a written assessment of some sort. Some Practitioner courses run over a shorter period of time and require students to complete reading and study modules before attending one or two weekend workshops. Such courses can lack the practice and feedback elements of the more traditional 15-day Practitioner course.

*Master Practitioner* – These courses typically run over several months and in addition to the formal training and practice they will usually require a project or dissertation to be undertaken by the student. Typically, a student would take a Master Practitioner course after completing Practitioner level certification and with at least 18 months of NLP practice as a foundation to build upon. Again, a typical minimum of 15 days formal classroom training is common for this level of certification.

*Trainer* – These courses, for those who have already achieved Master Practitioner accreditation, typically run over 21 days and will qualify you to run your own accredited NLP training courses and issue NLP Diploma, Practitioner and, in some cases, Master Practitioner certificates.

# CHOOSING AN NLP COURSE

There are many reasons why you might want to pursue a NLP training course or gain a formal NLP certification. It can be helpful to be clear about your own specific outcomes before choosing a course, as most courses have a particular emphasis or set of principles some of which will suit your outcomes better than others. Whilst some courses appear to offer levels of certification for lesser (or greater) financial expenditure or taught hours of training, others, perhaps without any formal accreditation, might offer a particular focus on personal development, business or coaching applications, or come with a personal recommendation or a high profile trainer with a name in the NLP training industry that is of particular interest to you.

It is helpful to ask yourself what your outcomes are and to have a clear vision of what you would like to see, hear and feel once you have completed your course. Whatever course you choose it is likely to involve considerable input of your financial, intellectual, emotional and time resources – so it is a good idea to be clear about what you want to get back from this investment in yourself before you embark on any such program. In addition to reading all that you can about the course it is a good idea to speak to previous participants and ask them what they got from the program and whether they think it would help you reach your outcomes. If possible, also speak to the trainers themselves to get a good understanding and feel for their own emphasis, style and principles.

Another point to consider is how you best like to learn. Do you prefer to learn by reading and studying or by interacting and practising new skills with others? Clearly, much of NLP is about how we interact and experience other people so a course which is mostly 'distance learning' or one which involves being trained as part of a large audience without the opportunity to interact with other individuals or in small groups might lack some of the opportunities to practise and develop the skills that working in a smaller group with a higher trainer to student ratio can bring. Courses that have high trainer to student ratios and involve more time interacting and practising with others are usually more expensive both in terms of time and money than those which rely heavily on distance learning or training large audiences.

# Creating Success series

The above titles are available from all good bookshops.
For further information on these and other Kogan Page titles,
or to order online, visit the Kogan Page website at
www.koganpage.com